MAPPING CONQUEST

Baggage
Line of Battle
Reserve

Mapping Conquest

The Battle Maps of Horseshoe Bend

KATHRYN H. BRAUND

The University of Georgia Press *Athens*

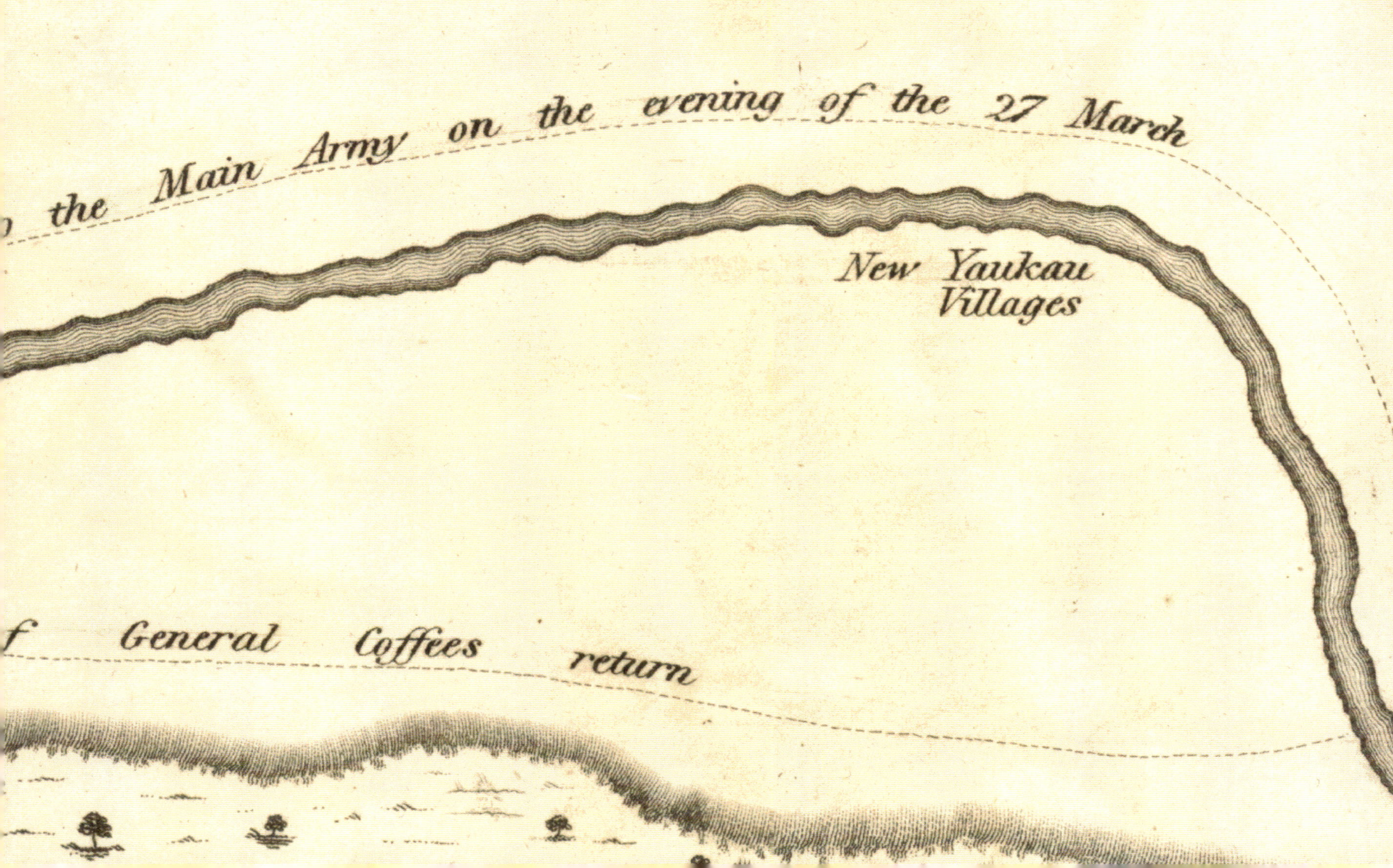

This publication is made possible in part through a grant from the Bradley Hale Fund for Southern Studies.

Athens, Georgia 30602
www.ugapress.org

Designed by Erin Kirk
Set in Adobe Caslon Pro
Printed and bound by Friesens
The paper in this book meets the guidelines for permanence and durability of the Committee on Production Guidelines for Book Longevity of the Council on Library Resources.

Most University of Georgia Press titles are available from popular e-book vendors.

Printed in Canada
28 27 26 25 24 C 5 4 3 2 1

Library of Congress Cataloging-in-Publication Data

Names: Braund, Kathryn E. Holland, 1955– author.
Title: Mapping conquest : the battle maps of Horseshoe Bend / Kathryn H. Braund.
Other titles: Battle maps of Horseshoe Bend
Description: Athens, Georgia : The University of Georgia Press, [2024] | Includes bibliographical references and index.
Identifiers: LCCN 2023058436 | ISBN 9780820366845 (hardback)
Subjects: LCSH: Horseshoe Bend, Battle of, Ala., 1814—Maps. | Horseshoe Bend, Battle of, Ala., 1814. | Creek War, 1813–1814—Campaigns—Maps. | Creek Indians—Alabama—History. | Cartographers—Alabama.
Classification: LCC E83.813 .B73 2024 | DDC 973.5/2380223—dc23/eng/20240214
LC record available at https://lccn.loc.gov/2023058436

Contents

Illustrations

Documents

Preface

This book began as an attempt to locate information about the Battle of Horseshoe Bend, the terminal battle of the Creek War of 1813–1814. Several maps of the battlefield are well known, but information about their creation and their creators is confused or lacking and, in some cases, incorrect. Although a few have been published, they have not been subjected to scrutiny or analysis. The search for information about the maps led me to the discovery of many others, mostly small hand-drawn maps by American soldiers who participated in the battle and a number of engraved maps published in the decades following the war. The number of maps I found astounded me given the paucity of manuscript or published maps of Creek War battles and spurred me to research the men who created them and the meaning they attempted to convey with their maps.

By the early nineteenth century, professionally produced manufactured maps were increasingly popular in America. With the outbreak of war with Britain in 1812, commercial maps were available for purchase nationwide. Interest in the war resulted in a growing demand for details about battles and troop movements. Maps portraying the "seat of war" appeared in newspaper accounts of events and as printed sheets. Perhaps the best remembered were published by John Melish, who produced a series of sheet maps depicting the "theater" of the war in various locales as well as an atlas.[1] The success of Melish's publications—he sold so many that he had to replace the plate used for engraving his *Map of the Seat of War in North America*—testifies to the importance that Americans placed on maps as adjuncts to written descriptions to elucidate military movements and battles. Avidly consumed during the war, the prevalence and popularity of commercially produced engraved maps was no doubt a spur to the amateur cartographers in Andrew Jackson's army, who produced their own maps after their battle at Horseshoe Bend.

The efforts of Jackson's cartographers (as well as their creative interpretation by commercial mapmakers) also contributed to the many maps depicting events in the Creek War after the fact. No doubt Jackson's stunning success at Horseshoe Bend and his status as an unparalleled war hero after the Battle of New Orleans helped propel sales of such maps in the postwar era, including *Map of the Seat of War among the Creek Indians from the Original Drawing in the War Department*, which appeared in Melish's *Military and Topographical Atlas*, published in 1815.[2]

The manuscript maps produced by the American soldiers at Horseshoe Bend were not the products of professional cartographers or mass-produced productions aimed at general consumers. Rather, they represented a novel attempt at graphic communication as soldiers tried to help colleagues, friends, and family visualize their experience at war by providing sketches to accompany their written and verbal descriptions of the battle. Although the maps were personal testimony to the important event of March 27, 1814, the mapmakers focused on their shared experience as part of an army rather than their personal

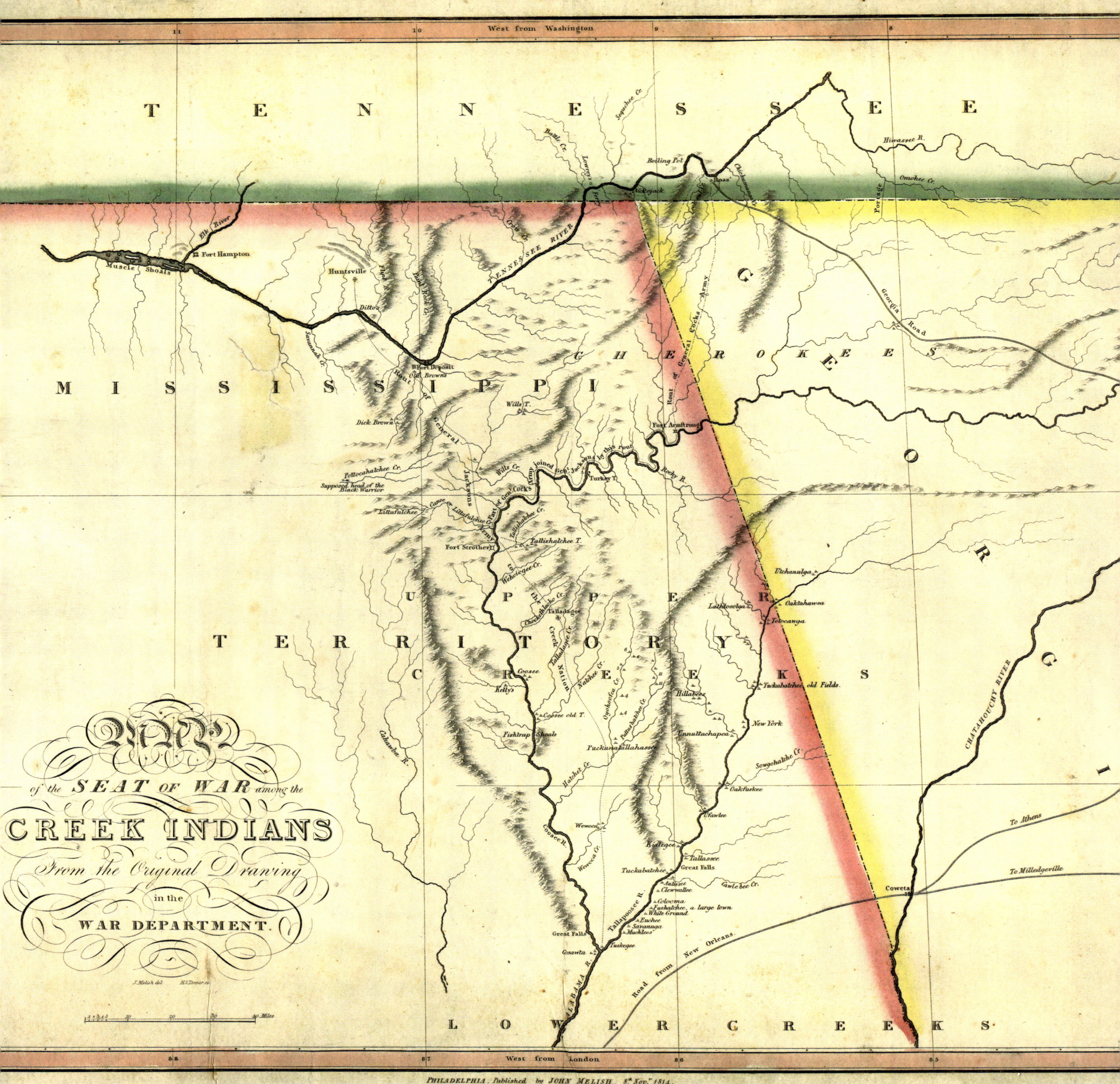

PHILADELPHIA. Published by JOHN MELISH, 8th Nov.r 1814.

participation. The maps include the same essential elements, expressed in a variety of styles with varying emphasis. All focus on the American army's experience. The personal and poignant individual experiences of the men were sometimes relegated to the letters that accompanied their maps, but most often, letters home recounted the story of the army's success rather than discussing the details of individual participation.

Although a study of the maps and their American soldier creators—as well as those published later—would seem to skew our vision of the battle, the opposite is true. These valuable productions, if one ponders them with intensity, reveal considerable details about the Americans' opponents: the Red Stick Creek Indians who chose the battle site based on topographic features and constructed a fortification that continues to impress and fascinate us as much as it dominates the maps. We have no Creek maps or direct personal accounts of the battle. Thus, any evidence provided by the mapmakers of March 27 is valuable in revealing the Creek side of the story.

Although my study of maps associated with the War of 1812 is in no way exhaustive, I was both surprised and perplexed at the number of manuscript maps depicting the Battle of Horseshoe Bend compared with other battles in the Creek War—and indeed the War of 1812 itself. The only other Creek War battle map is a single manuscript map of Talladega and a manuscript sketch of Fort Mims produced after the battle that situates the fortification in the landscape and points out prominent locations associated with the attack.[3] My efforts to uncover Creek War battle maps will, I hope, lead to the discovery of even more maps and increase knowledge about the Battle of Horseshoe Bend and the Creek War in general as well as engender respect and appreciation for cartographic art in its many manifestations.

Taken together, the many manuscript maps of the Horseshoe battleground provide new insights into the battle. Careful study of this rich cartographic record reveals powerful stories about the cartographers who produced them, the battle of the Horseshoe, and what it meant to the American victors. They allow us to focus on the army's movement as a whole as well as tease out the place of individuals who participated, even those who remain anonymous. Together with the strong documentary record of the battle, they provide a new way of "seeing" the battle both spatially and temporally and communicating the meaning of the engagement both for the participants and historically. More importantly, they focus attention on the fortification built by the Red Stick Creeks to repel the American invaders, providing insight into Creek battle preparation and strategy.

The maps did more than merely record the actions of an army attacking fortified enemy location. For the makers, their maps served as records of their participation and knowledge of the most important American victory of the war. That victory in their view was made possible by honorable action of officers and men. Their maps reflected their pride in their army's achievement and served as tangible memorials to the effort.

Along with maps, this volume features an extensive collection of letters and documents written by participants or other close observers. Taken together, the maps and documents allow readers the opportunity for careful study and reflection. The transcriptions of manuscript letters and documents presented here retain original spelling, capitalization, and punctuation

FIGURE 1. John Melish's *Map of the Seat of War among the Creek Indians from the Original Drawing in the War Department* inaccurately portrayed Jackson's route to the conflux of the Coosa and Tallapoosa Rivers and omitted the battle site at Cholocco Litabixee (Horse's Flat Foot) or Horseshoe Bend. Most of the major Creek towns as well as some of the American forts built during the war are shown with a fair degree of accuracy. Courtesy of the American Philosophical Society.

with as much fidelity as possible. Flourishes and repeated words have been deleted. To aid clarity, missing words or letters are occasionally supplied in square brackets. Superscripts have been dropped to the line for readability. For manuscript letters, interlineations have been included as the writer intended while strikethroughs are omitted. People mentioned in the letters are identified if possible, either by the insertion of full name in square brackets or in a footnote. Quotations in the first four chapters from original documents included in this volume adhere to the style listed above, with citations to repositories and major published versions also included in footnotes for the reader's convenience.

Acknowledgments

I would like to thank Ove Jensen, who, while serving as head of interpretation at Horseshoe Bend National Military Park (HOBE), secured my assistance in locating documents associated with the battle and the park. It was the beginning of a decade of research about the battle and led me to the maps featured here. I learned much from Ove's knowledge of military history and that of the park. Along the way, a host of other HOBE staff members both informed me and listened to my ramblings about their park and I am particularly grateful to Heather Tassin and Matthew Robinson in that regard. In addition to park personnel, I have enjoyed conversations with fellow students of the battle, many of whom make up the dedicated membership of the Friends of Horseshoe Bend, an all-volunteer organization that supports the park's educational mission. Among that number are Harold Banks, Ralph Banks, Greg Wilson, T. R. Henderson, Brian Conary, and the late John C. Hall. From the academic world, I am grateful for discussions with my friend and colleague Gregory A. Waselkov, archaeologist, ethnohistorian, and expert on the Creek War; Tom Kanon, now retired from the Tennessee State Archives; David and Jeanne Heidler, longtime friends who have published widely on Jackson and his era; and Tom Coens and Daniel Feller, editors of *The Papers of Andrew Jackson* at the University of Tennessee. I would also like to thank Suzanne LaRosa, whose encouragement and support were invaluable. I would especially like to thank my husband, Kyle G. Braund, for his steadfast encouragement and support

Many repositories and organizations have been gracious in responding to my research requests and assisted me in a variety of ways, and for their help, I am very grateful. I would especially like to thank those who provided and granted permission for the use of illustrations, particularly Mrs. Ann Cousins and Kenneth Boone as well as staff members at the Alabama Archaeological Society, the Alabama Department of Archives and History, the American Philosophical Society, the Birmingham Public Library, the Gilder Lehrman Institute of American History, the High Museum of Art, Horseshoe Bend National Military Park, the Library of Congress, the Mississippi Department of Archives and History, the North Carolina State Archives, the National Park Service, the Tennessee Historical Society, the Tennessee State Library and Archives, and the Special Collections at the University of Tennessee.

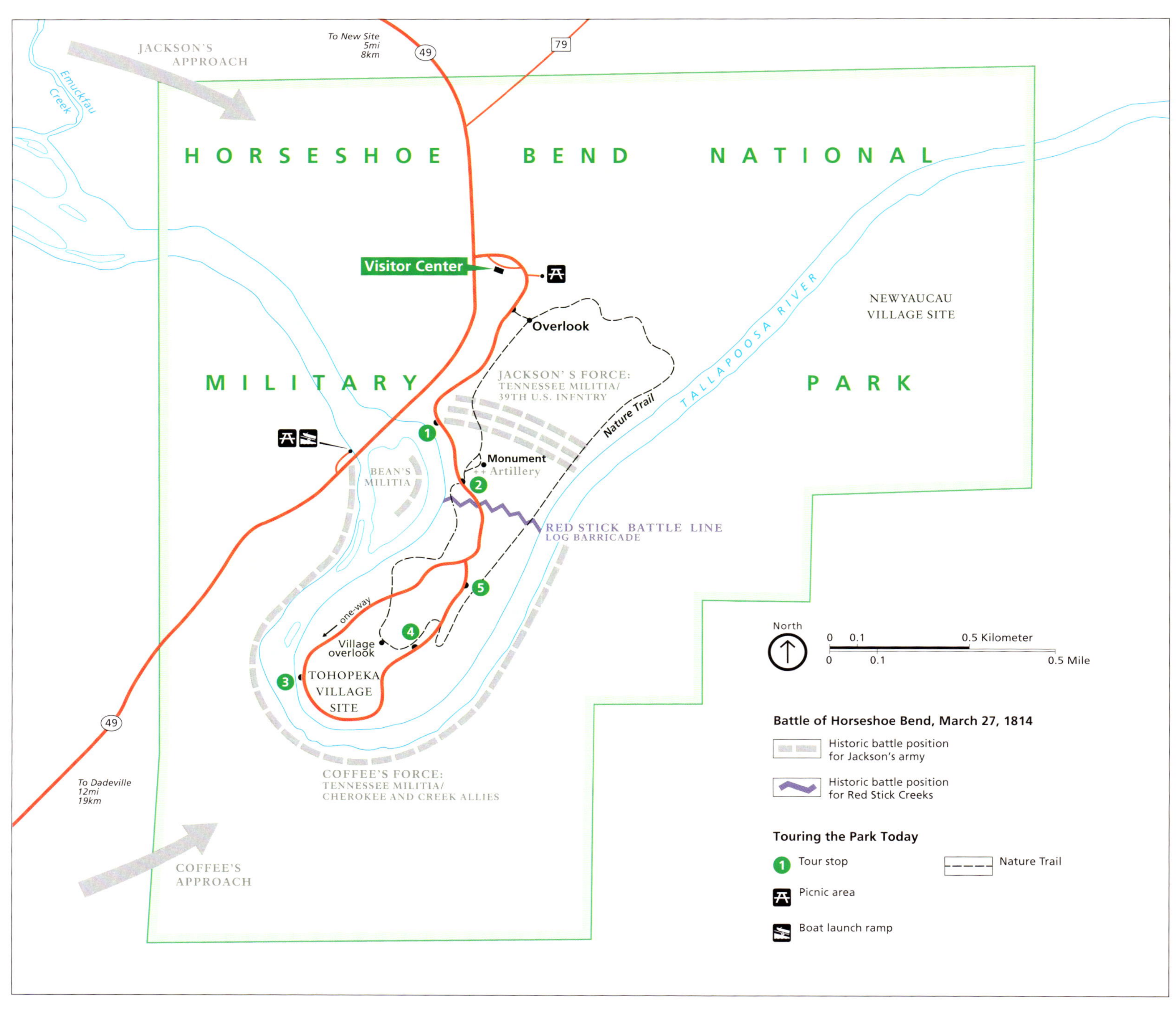

FIGURE 2. The battle site is preserved today as Horseshoe Bend National Military Park. Courtesy of Horseshoe Bend National Military Park, National Park Service.

MAPPING CONQUEST

Chain of

Newyorcau an old Town

Coffees Brig of Horse men

Tohoopeca

Spies

Cherokees

Cherokees crossed the River

a Small

Bend of the River

Island

Russels Spies & Cherokees

Coffees Brigade of Horse

Breast Work

Front Guard

39th Regt U.S. Inft

E. & W. 3 M

CHAPTER 1

The Battle of Horseshoe Bend *The Maps and Their Makers*

On March 27, 1814, an American army led by General Andrew Jackson approached a fortified position in a large bend of the Tallapoosa River in the heart of Creek country. There, Jackson's allied forces engaged the Red Sticks, as the enemy Creek Indians were known. The site, known as Tohopeka, which means "fortification" in the Muskogee language, is best known today as Horseshoe Bend. The epic battle lasted through the day and proved to be one of the deadliest in American history.

The Creek War had begun as an internal conflict, with an attack on the Creek National Council by insurgents, who symbolically raised the "red stick of war" against their own leadership. They attacked and killed "old" chiefs who, acceding to American demands, had tried to avoid war by executing those who had openly attacked Americans along Creek borders and in the heart of the Creek Nation. Most important, the insurgents laid siege to Tuckabatchee, one of the largest and most important Upper Creek towns and seat of the National Council, a relatively new body that managed Creek relations with the United States. The outbreak of civil war among the Creek Indians spread panic in the Mississippi Territory and into Tennessee and Georgia, as settlers feared the Creek troubles would result in widespread frontier violence and merge into the ongoing war against Britain, who many believed would encourage and support attacks against American settlements. In the Tensaw region, Creeks and Americans alike "forted up" fearing attacks by the Red Sticks. In July 1813, Red Sticks visited Spanish Pensacola to obtain arms and ammunition for their attacks against Tuckabatchee. Mississippi territorial militia, seeking to prevent an escalation of hostilities, attacked the Red Stick supply caravan returning from Pensacola near Burnt Corn Creek. The insurgents retaliated with an attack on the Samuel Mims plantation in the Mobile-Tensaw Delta, at the intersection of American, Spanish, and Creek territory on August 30, 1813. There, American settlers and Creeks opposed to the Red Sticks had fortified themselves and welcomed protection from the Mississippi territorial militia. The ferocious and spectacularly successful assault by some 700 Red Sticks destroyed the compound, killed around 250 of the fort's inhabitants, and saw nearly 100 survivors, mainly women and enslaved African Americans, taken captive by the victorious Red Sticks. "Remember Fort Mims" became an American battle cry and the "Creek War" became a major adjunct to America's larger 1812 war against the British.[1]

Following the attack on Fort Mims, Americans quickly cobbled together armies for a three-pronged attack on the Creek Nation. Members and supporters of the National Council actively sought American aid against the Red Stick rebels and many fought alongside the Americans as allies. From the Mississippi Territory, troops moved up the Alabama River with the assistance of Choctaw Indians and achieved a major American victory at Eccanachaca (Holy Ground) in late December 1813. Georgia troops headed west and were saved from destruction in early 1814 at Calabee Creek by their allies, National Creek soldiers under the command of Major Timpoochee Barnard.

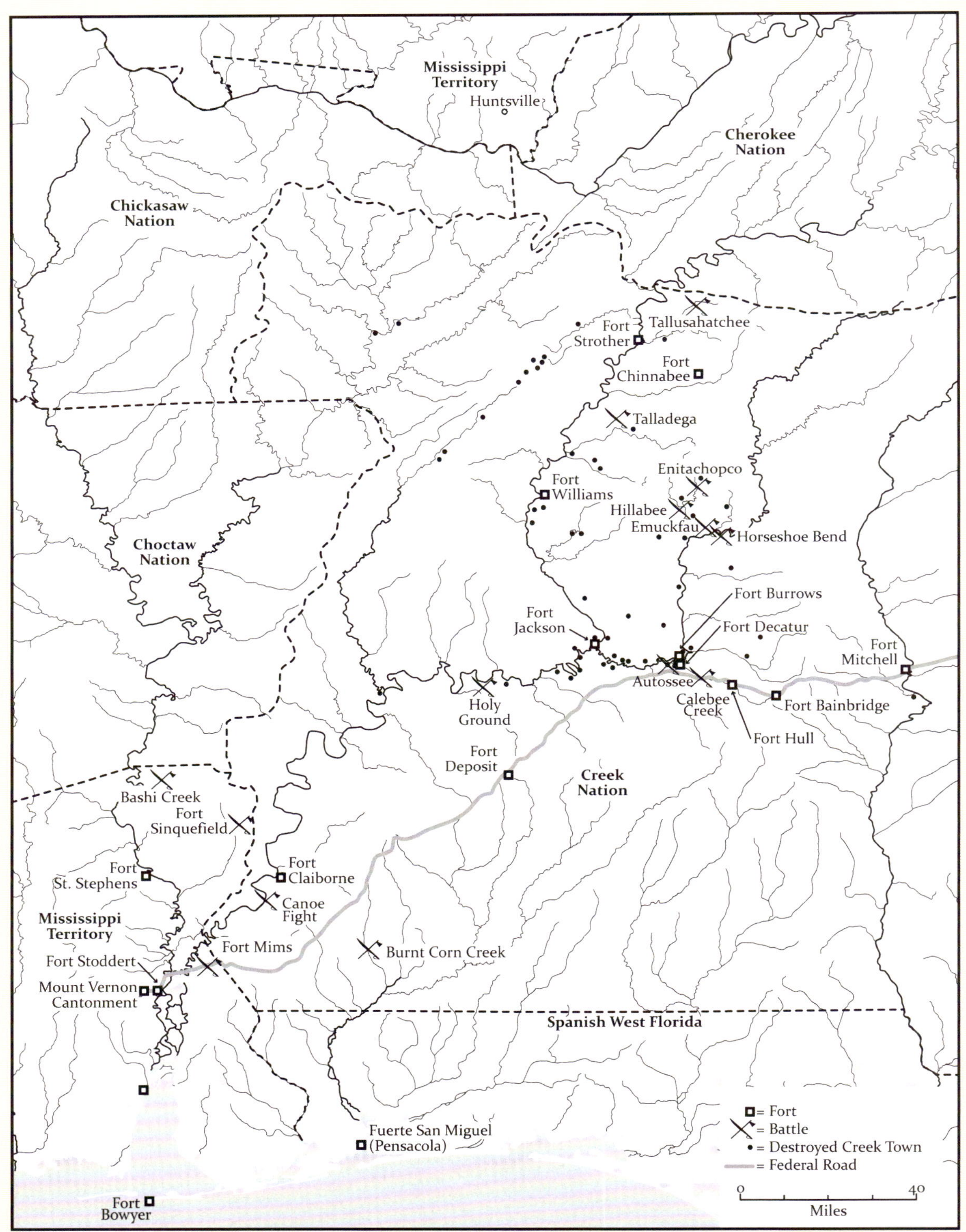

FIGURE 3. Battlefields and forts of the Creek War, adapted from *General Jackson's Campaign against the Creek Indians, 1813 and 1814*. Map by Sarah Mattics, Center for Archaeological Studies, University of South Alabama.

From the north, Tennesseans were reinforced by Cherokees and guided into the heart of the Creek Nation by Creek National Council interpreters and "spies" who gathered intelligence on Red Sticks and provided other valuable information on routes and locations. By the time Jackson reached the barricaded river bend in March 1814, his forces had engaged the Red Sticks in a variety of situations: attacking and capturing villages that offered no resistance (Litafuchee and Hillabee), destroying villages that offered resistance (Tallushatchee), rescuing members of the Creek National Council under siege by Red Sticks (Talladega), and failing to deliver knockout blows in engagements in the heart of the Upper Creek Nation (Emuckfau and Enitachopco) in January 1814.

During the engagement at Emuckfau Creek, General John Coffee was dispatched to burn a fortification American spies had reported at Horseshoe Bend, but Coffee discovered the defenses there were too stout for his limited force. Emuckfau was a hard-fought engagement during which the Red Sticks attacked Jackson's fortified camp three times and left his army frazzled and fatigued. Two days later, on their return to their base at Fort Strother, the Red Sticks attacked again as the army was crossing Enitachopco Creek. Part of Jackson's line failed, but an extraordinary effort by the cannon crew bought the Americans enough time to regroup and drive off the attackers. The Red Sticks had nearly secured a major victory over the Americans.[2]

Following the near disasters at Emuckfau and Enitachopco, Jackson beefed up his numbers and worked to instill discipline among his troops. By the morning of March 27, he commanded the largest coalition force of the conflict, three thousand of whom he marched to Horseshoe Bend.[3] His army was composed of Tennessee militia units, newly recruited volunteer units, five hundred Cherokee Indians, and about one hundred allied Creek Indians under the command of William McIntosh. Most significantly, the newly organized Thirty-Ninth United States Infantry Regiment added about six hundred disciplined and trained troops to his numbers. At Tohopeka, the American attackers faced about a thousand Red Sticks; men from the Creek towns of Okfuskee, Okchai, Nuyaka, Hillabee, Fish Ponds, and Eufaula; as well as a substantial number of noncombatants residing in the village behind the barricade. As Jackson surmised, the Red Sticks had "the utmost confidence upon their strength—their situation—& and the assurances of their prophets, they calculated on repulsing us with great ease."[4]

As the Americans approached, Coffee led the mounted men and Indian allies across the Tallapoosa to encircle the river bend while the rest of the army moved into position facing the Creek barricade. Jackson's artillery planted two small cannons, and by midmorning, the assault on the barricade began. Heavy fire from the American cannon failed to breach the four-hundred-yard-long log structure protecting the defenders, a fortification that was according to the attackers, "admirably calculated for defence."[5] It was not until Cherokee Indians managed to cross the Tallapoosa and engage the Red Sticks from the rear that Americans were able to swarm the walls and begin the bloody business of destroying their enemies.

The battle, which began around 10:00 a.m., did not end until darkness fell and virtually every Red Stick was dead. No record was made of the dead or wounded women and children, but there were, according to a note by one of the officers, "too many." It was the largest and last battle in the Creek War and also the largest loss of life by Native Americans in any battle against armies of the United States before or since.[6]

The morning after the battle was hectic. Moving across the peninsula and stepping over the corpses of the slain, Jackson's officers were employed in a number of tasks, including counting the dead enemy, which they reportedly did by cutting off the tips of their noses.[7] Some troops were dispatched to capture or kill sixteen or so wounded Red Sticks who had taken refuge in the overhanging banks next to the river and who refused to surrender (or perhaps were so badly wounded they were unable to do so).[8] Other Americans were employed in weighing down and sinking their own dead in the river and concealing the site of the one land burial of a dead American: that of Major Lemuel Purnell Montgomery.[9] There were Creek women, children, and elders to attend to as well. Many were wounded; all were dazed and scared. Cherokee soldiers claimed some of these women as their slaves and left the battleground. Officers and Jackson's small corps of physicians attended to the American wounded

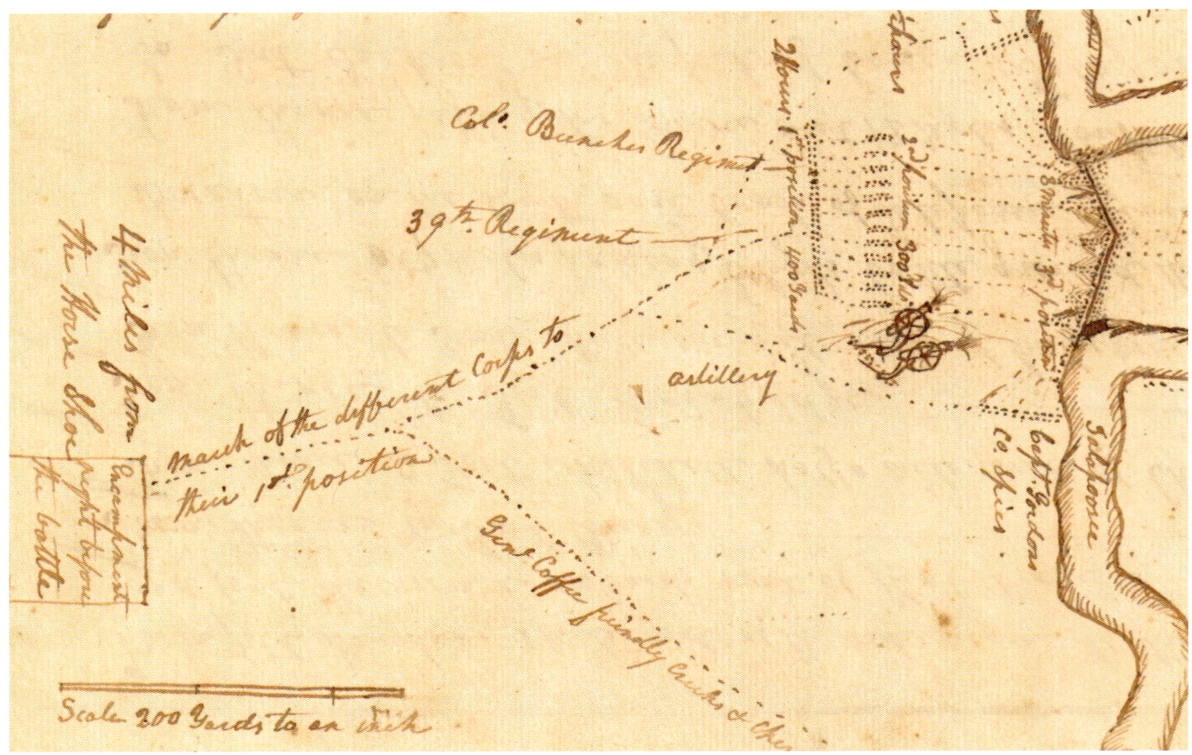

FIGURE 4. Detail from the map attributed to Colonel William Carroll illustrating the line of march and deployment of the artillery. Courtesy of the State Archives of North Carolina, North Carolina Department of Natural and Cultural Resources.

while enlisted men were tasked with building litters to evacuate them. As the acrid smoke from the smoldering barricade hovered over the bend, many of the victorious Americans walked the battle-ravaged landscape. Some, like Third Lieutenant Robert H. McEwen, sat down to produce a "description of the battle ground" and to record their "memorandums." (See figure 6.)

McEwen's "description" was actually a pen-and-ink manuscript map. McEwen's map, like the other known manuscript maps of the battle, was a small sketch, mainly done "by eye."[10] Even John A. Cheatham, Jackson's topographical engineer, only bothered to plot the main topographic features (the river bend and enemy fortification) to scale.[11] These small maps were folded and carried in pocket notebooks or enclosed in letters sent home to family and friends, sent directly to newspapers, or enclosed with official battle reports. Most were drafted in the immediate aftermath of battle by members of the officer corps. Although having so many maps depicting this famous battle is a boon to scholarship, the large number produced does raise the question of why. Why did so many American soldiers decide to produce maps of this battlefield when other Creek War battles—indeed, other War of

FIGURE 5 (*opposite*). Detail from Carroll's map indicating the location of the river crossing by the allied Cherokee and Creek regiments, along with details about their horses and the location of the "covering party of whites." Courtesy of the State Archives of North Carolina.

New Yauca
or Horse Shoe
Town
Talapoosee
River
Town
8 minutes 3rd position
2nd position 300 Yds
1¼ hours
Capt. Gordons
Co. Spies
Corp Spies
1814
Carroll
J. Graham

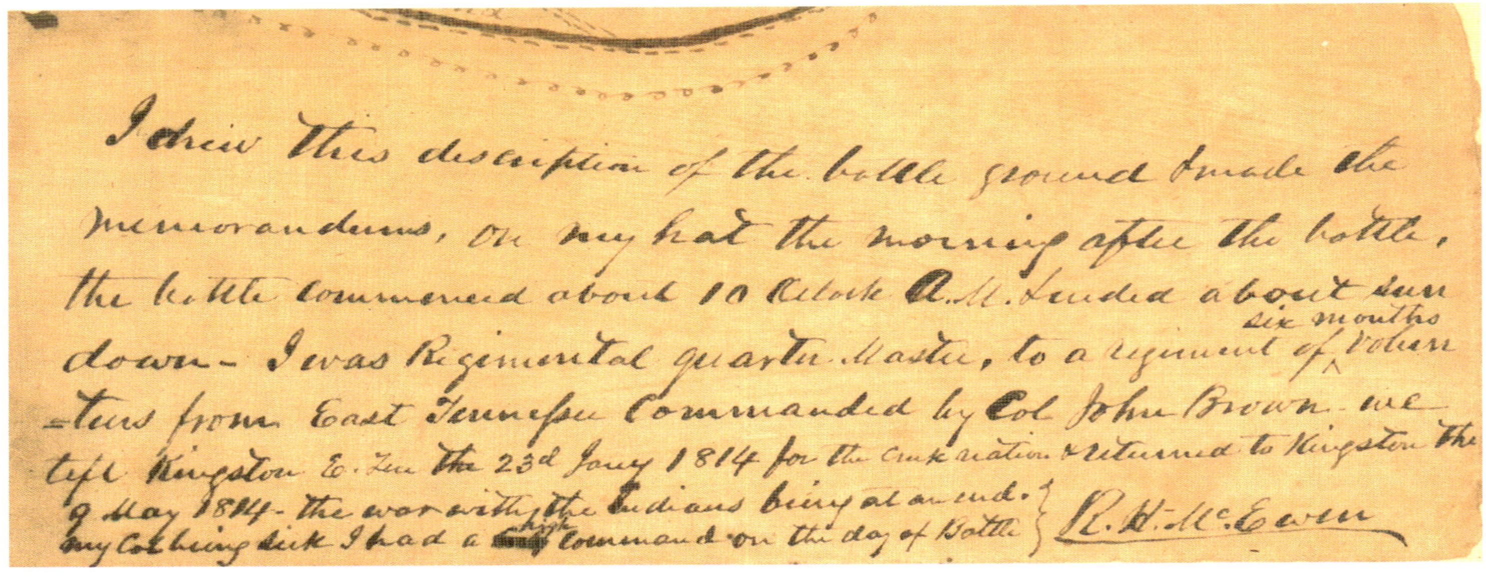

I drew this description of the battle ground & made the
memorandums, on my hat the morning after the battle.
the battle commenced about 10 OClock A.M. & ended about sun
down— I was Regimental quarter Master, to a regiment of six months Volun
-teers from East Tennessee Commanded by Col John Brown. we
left Kingston E. Ten the 23d Jany 1814 for the Creek nation & returned to Kingston the
9 May 1814— the war with the Indians being at an end.
my Col being sick I had a high command on the day of Battle } R. H. McEwen

FIGURE 6. R. H. McEwen's notation on his map of the Battle of Horseshoe Bend. Courtesy of the Library of Congress, Geography and Map Division.

1812 battles—were not similarly memorialized by participants?[12] The unique and compelling nature of the large river bend and the extraordinary Creek defensive work presented a memorable setting and one easy to render and that no doubt contributed to the production of maps. The Red Stick barricade, an unusual and formidable defensive work, occupies the central place on all the maps. Yet all the maps render the structure differently, raising another puzzling why. The scale of the military operation and the massive destruction of life witnessed by the participants made the epic event worthy of documentation. But neither the suitability of the terrain, the massive fortification they encountered, nor the monumental experience fully explain the flurry of amateur maps produced after the battle. To answer these questions, a closer look at the maps and their makers is essential. Unfortunately, not all the maps have been utilized or even consulted by scholars studying the battle. Thus, essential information about the defensive work, key to understanding and interpreting the battle, has scarcely been considered. Most important, the maps provide insight into Creek military strategy and help focus attention on the ultimate goal of the Red Stick Creek defenders as well as that of the American attackers.

The best-known map of the battle was produced by Captain John A. Cheatham, a twenty-three-year-old from Nashville who was appointed as assistant topographical engineer two weeks before the battle.[13] Cheatham had joined the war effort in January 1814 as part of Thomas Johnson's brigade.[14] Cheatham's signed map now resides in the National Archives. Cheatham measured both the river bend and Red Stick breastwork and rendered them "a scale of 400 yards to the Inch" while the rest of the map "was done by the eye."[15] Jackson dispatched a report to Major General Thomas Pinckney from "the Battle ground on bend of the Tallapoosa" the day after the battle and noted that he enclosed "a hasty sketch taken by the eye of the situation in which the enemy were encamped, & of the manner in which I approached them." This map, not conclusively identified or located, was likely a preliminary sketch by John Cheatham that served as the basis for his more polished map.[16] The Cheatham map is no doubt the one Jackson sent to General Pinckney on

FIGURE 7. Map by Colonel John A. Cheatham. Courtesy of the National Archives and Records Administration.

The untitled map carries the following top note: "The bend and fortification of the enemy is plotted by a scale of 400 yards to the Inch the balance was done by eye." Unlike the other maps, Cheatham provided orientation "N" and "S." The map notes the route of the army's march to the site as well as Coffee's route around the peninsula and return to the main army after the battle. Of interest, in his key, he notes the "Indian huts" in toe of the bend were newly constructed. As do several of the maps, Cheatham marked the campsite of the army the night before the battle "Camp on the night of the 26th March 1814" and the site of the previous engagement at Emuckfau, "Battle ground of Emuckfau on the 22 January 1814." His delineation of the "high ground" both inside and along the curvature of the bend compares favorably with modern topographic maps. Bleed through from the verso, which reads, "Map of battle ground Jackson over the Creeks the 27th March 1814," can be discerned near the island.

The key reads as follows:

Explanation

A	represents the hill from which our cannon played upon the enemys works—
//////	represents high broken Piney ridges, and broken ground, between which and the river is level flat land—
- - - - -	represents our men drawn up in line of battle at different points—
□□□□	represents Indian huts, and village, all of which was new—

J. A. Cheatham, A. Topl. Engineer

April 5, noting it was "a plan somewhat more correct than that which I forwarded you from the battleground."[17]

An almost identical copy of the Cheatham map, unsigned but in the same handwriting, was forwarded by William Bradford to General William Henry Harrison on April 5, 1814.[18] Bradford, an engineer with the Seventeenth U.S. Infantry, had been ordered to Jackson's army by his commanding officer, Colonel William P. Anderson. During the battle, Bradford served as the principal engineer and commanded the artillery that pounded the barricade. His letter to Harrison was a request for reassignment to Harrison's forces at the conclusion of the Creek campaign and included an account of the battle along with "a map of that part of the river occupied by the savages, together with Genl. Jackson's order of the line of march."[19] This map is notable for its "line of march" diagram on the document's reverse side.

The Mississippi Department of Archives and History holds "Hugh Ervin's Map of the Battle of Horseshoe Bend, 1814." A note on the verso explains the map is a "Drawing of my fathers in the war of 1812."[20] This is presumably Hugh Irvin, who was a private in Carson's Regiment of Mississippi Militia.[21] Whoever sent the map to the Mississippian obtained the assistance of John Cheatham, for the map was copied from Cheatham's, although not precisely, and there are additional details not included on the Cheatham map. An incomplete map owned by the Library of Congress more closely resembles this map than Cheatham's other two productions but carries no annotations.

FIGURE 8 (*opposite*). Reverse side of William Bradford's map detailing the "enclosed square" employed by Jackson's troops when they made camp on campaign as well as the line of march with artillery wagons toward the battleground. The front of the map is nearly identical to the Cheatham map and in Cheatham's hand. Courtesy of the Library of Congress, Manuscript Division, William Henry Harrison Papers.

The key reads as follows:

- - -	Represents the line of fires in the encampment.
o-o-o-o	Represents the troops when formed in Camp.
oooo	Represents the troops when in line of march.
♯	Represents the artillery & wagons on the line of march.

[Enclosed in letter of April 5th 1814. Wm Bradford to Wm H Harrison]

--- Represents the line of fires in the encampment.

ooo Represents the troops when formed in Camp.

ooo Represents the troops when in line of March.

Represents the artillery & waggons on the line of March

942

FIGURE 9. Hugh Ervin's map of the Battle of Horseshoe Bend. Courtesy of the Archives and Records Services Division, Mississippi Department of Archives and History.

In addition to a key, labeled "Representations," Ervin provided the army's "track" to the battlefield from their campsite near Emuckfau and used a variety of symbols to represent topographical features as well as the movement and position of the American troops and "Indian huts." On the lower left corner, a faded and nearly illegible notation indicates the position of Coffee's "Picket Guard" stationed on the "[probable] trace from the Oakfuskey Towns." Ervin used rectangles as the symbol for "Indian huts" to indicate the village in the toe of the bend and the burned village of Nuyaka. He also placed four on the lower east side of the river bend. The notation accompanying the symbols is damaged and obscured by a fold line but seems to indicate "huts on the river bend," the only document to indicate the presence of structures outside the bend or the town. Another remark unique to Ervin's map is a notation marked by the rectangular symbol between Emuckfau Creek and the site of Jackson's camp on the 26th of a "Camp Look out 22nd of January 1814," indicating the battle site of Emuckfau.

The key reads as follows:

REPRESENTATIONS

A	Represents the Hill from which the artillery was played
' ' ' ' ' ' '	Represents Mountains & broken ground
- - - -	Represents men formed in line of battle
. . . . .	Represents the Line of March
□□□	Represents the Indian huts

March 27th 1814

Picket Guard

Trace from the Oakfuskey Towns

Gen'l Coffee's track attempting to cross the river

New Yorker Village

Representation

was pt

Represents the Hill from which the ...

Represents Mountains & broken ground

Represents men drawn in line of battle

Represents the line of March

Represents the Indian huts

Two other frequently reproduced maps of the battle are problematic due to identification issues. The first, a map frequently attributed to Andrew Jackson, is owned by the Tennessee Historical Society and titled *Battle of Tehopiska*. The map was donated to the society along with Jackson's original report on the battle to Governor Willie Blount.[22] The two documents were found years after the Creek War in a derelict building once used by the governor as an office and presented to General W. A. Quarles of Clarksville, Tennessee. The two documents were then bound in a handsome folder and presented by Quarles's nephew to the Tennessee Historical Society in 1884. The report and an engraved facsimile of the manuscript map were first published in 1899 in the *American Historical Magazine*. The editor stated that the report was in Jackson's handwriting and included the cryptic notation "the map is a facsimile of the original map drawn by General Jackson." But the manuscript map found with the report is not in Jackson's handwriting.[23] The map, like the report, shows evidence of being trifolded and enclosed in an envelope. The map's verso bears the notation "Genl Jackson March 31st 1814." Whether the map was indeed enclosed with the report or acquired later by Blount remains a mystery, but there is little doubt that the map was not drawn by Jackson himself.[24] The small, elegant production is notable for its use of blue ink. It is here referred to as the "Jackson map," despite problems with its authorship and provenance.

FIGURE 10 (*opposite*). "Battle of Tehopiska," known as Andrew Jackson's map. The map displays prominent terrain features including the river, island, and high ground of the battlefield as well as the placement of all troops, equipment, and prominent landmarks, such as the Nuyaka village, the site of the previous battle of Emuckfau, and notably, "that angle at which Mongomery fell." From Major General Andrew Jackson's official report (with map) to Tennessee governor Willie Blount following the 1814 Battle of Horseshoe Bend, Andrew Jackson Collection, ID# 36423. Courtesy of the Tennessee Historical Society, Tennessee State Library and Archives.

The key reads as follows:

1	Coffee Cavalry	10	Waggons Pack horses & wounded in center
2	Cherokees	11	Col. Copeland
3	Indian Village	12	E. Ten Militia
4	High Grounds	13	Col. Cheatham
5	Breast Works	14	Rear Guard
6	Island	15	Emuckfau—Old battle ground
7	Advanced guard	16	New Youcau—burnt before
8	Hill & Artillery	17	High Hills
9	Regulars	o.	That angle at which Mongomery fell

1 Coffee Cavalry –
2 Cherokees –
3 Indian Village –
4 High Grounds –
5 Breast Works –
6 Island –
7 Advanced guard –
8 Hill & Artillery

9 Regulars
10 Waggons Pack horses & wounded in center
11 Col. Copeland
12 E. Ten. Militia
13 Col. Cheatham
14 Rear Guard

15 Emuckfau – Old battle ground –
16 New Youcau – burn[t] before –
17 High Hills –
0 – That angle at whi[ch] Mongomery fell –

The most dramatic of the maps, rendered in bold red and black ink, is owned by the Alabama Department of Archives and History. The map is untitled but bears the inscription "For Capt. Leonard L. Tarrants, Winchester W. Tenessee } J. L. Holmes."[25] Tarrants had been a private in Colonel Thomas H. Benton's Second Regiment of Tennessee Volunteer Infantry earlier in the war.[26] Tarrants is sometimes listed as the map's creator, but it seems clear the map is directed to him, presumably produced by Holmes. Lieutenant J. L. Holmes was in Captain Richard Sharp's company, part of Colonel Stephen Copeland's regiment, the Third Regiment of West Tennessee Militia.[27] Holmes's unit saw action at Horseshoe Bend. His exact relationship to Tarrants is unclear, but he either produced or procured the map for Tarrants.

FIGURE 11 (*opposite*). Map produced for Captain Leonard L. Tarrant. Courtesy of the Alabama Department of Archives and History.

The untitled map carries the following note at the base:

Battle Fought 27th March 1814
For Capt. Leonard L. Tarrants
Winchester W. Tenessee, } J. L. Holmes

Like most of the mapmakers, Holmes oriented his map from the perspective of the attackers. As a result, south is at the top of the map, north the bottom, east to the left, and west to the right. Holmes was obviously impressed by high, pine ridges ringing the bend detailing "A Craggy Chain of Hills" encircling the bend as well as "A Mountain Genl. Coffee's Stand." He notes "a small creek" leading down the "mountain" to the river as the area the "Spies & Cherokees crossed the River." Of interest is the symbol, in red, in the shape of a house, surrounded by irregular circles, indicating "Tehoopcau" village. He labeled the high ground of the peninsula as "Second Bend of the River" and added a line of dots that continue from the river crossing of the spies and Cherokee force to this "bend" of high ground. The red dots lining the "Breast Work" and throughout the peninsula represent Red Stick Creeks. Facing the "Breast Work," Holmes laid out the relative positions of the American forces. Behind the "Front Guard," he labeled the relative positions of the "39th Regt U. S. Inft.," a cannon drawing with the notation "Artillery," then E. & W. T[ennessee] M[ilitia]." He also located the "Baggage and Stores" as well as the "artillery wagon." "East. & West Tenssee Militia" followed by the "Rear Guard" also were placed on his map.

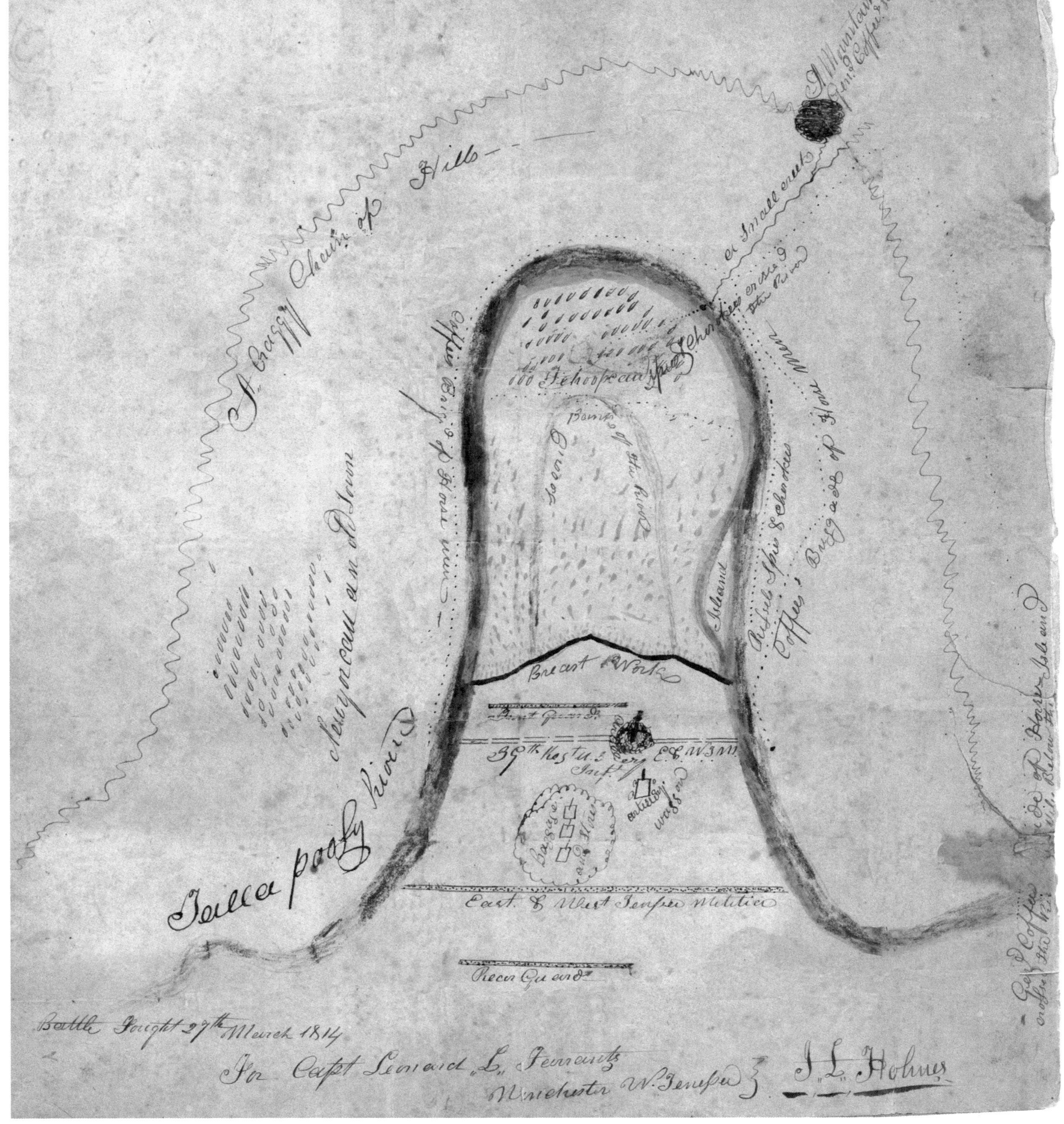

A Craggy Chain of Hills
Tallapoosy River
Breast Work
Island
Front Guard
Rear Guard
East & West Tenssee Militia
Battle Fought 27th March 1814
J. L. Holmes

A Tarrant is sometimes listed in secondary references as an officer in the Creek War, but he does not appear on any extant muster rolls of companies in action during the Creek War located to date. Benton's regiment was involved in the 1813 aborted Natchez expedition and discharged in April 1813. Thus, at the time of the battle at the Horseshoe, Tarrants should have been in Tennessee. The soldier's name on the map and pension records is rendered Tarrants.

Spelling aside, the map's owner was Leonard Tarrant, a resident of Winchester, Tennessee, who was married in September 1812 to Jane Estill.[28] The Tarrant family moved to Alabama following the Creek War, where he became a Methodist minister, served in the Alabama legislature, and was later a judge in Shelby County, Alabama. By 1832, he was acting as a subagent for the Creeks. When the agent, John Crowell, was relieved from duty in 1833, Tarrant was appointed as replacement. The map was donated to the Alabama Department of Archives and History in 1903 by Dr. Samuel H. Hogan, whose wife was Virginia C. Tarrant Hogan, the daughter of Leonard Tarrant.[29]

Equally well known is the map attributed to William Carroll. The striking map, which was sketched "a few days after the battle," resides among the papers of Joseph Graham, who commanded North and South Carolina regiments at the end of the Creek War. These troops were stationed at Fort Jackson, built on the site of the earlier French Fort Toulouse and the location of the treaty proceedings that ended the war.[30] The map includes an account of the battle on the reverse, with the last few lines running onto the map head, followed by a title "Battle of the Horshoe fought 27 March 1814 as scetched by Col^{o} Carroll (now Genl. Carroll) a few days after the battle." Neither the battle account nor the sketch are in Carroll's handwriting, and the title indicates the map was copied from the original after May 1814, the date of Carroll's promotion to major general of the Tennessee militia. In addition to this map, sketches of several Creek War–era forts are preserved in Graham's papers. These related plans and sketches have the same format as the Carroll map and were evidently done in the same hand, presumably by a member of Graham's staff.[31]

FIGURE 12. General Carroll's map, "Battle of the Horshoe fought 27 March 1814 as scetched by Colo. Carroll (now Genl. Carroll) a few days after the battle." Courtesy of the State Archives of North Carolina.

Carroll's map carries the following descriptive text on the reverse of the map, with the last line of the text carried over to the map itself:

> Battle of the Horse Shoe fought on 27 March 1814 Between Maj. General Jackson Commanding Genl. Coffee's Brigade about half of which were mounted men of west Tenessee & Colo. Bunches Regiment of east Tenesse Infantry 2 Companies of Spies and the 39th Regiment of United States Infantry commanded by Colo. Williams about 150 Cherokee Indians under Colo. Morgan of Knoxville and 80 friendly Creeks under McIntosh the half breed of Coweta making an effective force in the whole something upwards of 3000_______against the warriors of the Towns of New Yauca 2 towns of the Oakfuskees, Kealejah, Talasee, &c. &c. &c. suposed to be about 900 of the best warriors of the Creek Nation a number of the women & Children of the neighbouring towns were colected there from the confidence they had of it being a secure place—early in the morning 27 March 1814 General Jackson marched from his encampment 4 miles distant at 2 miles Genl. Coffees command filed to the right & crossed the Talapoosee 1½ miles below agreeably to previous arrangement the Spies, Artillery, Bunches & Williams Regiments, the Genl. & his staff took their positions in front of the works which extended from the River above to it below being composed of large logs laid one above the other from 5 to 8 feet high while the Infantry were in their 1st. & 2nd. position the artillery tryed to batter the logs

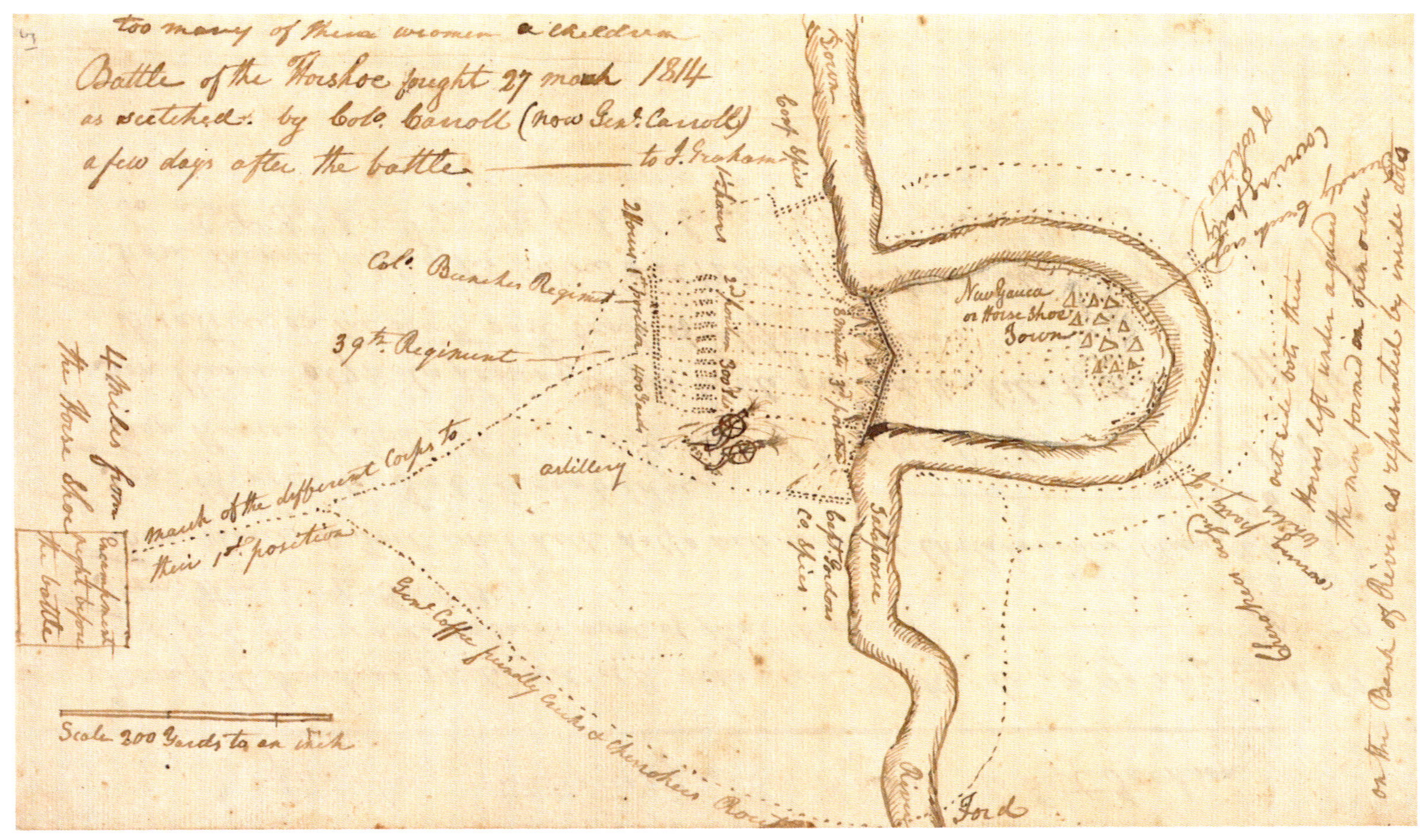

down but without effect The Infantry then charged from heads of sections in their 3 positions were 8 minutes before the[y] crossed the work. Jackson lost in the whole 26 killed 58 of wounded The hostile Indians 557 killed but too many of them women & children.

The map is devoid of a key but indicates the encampment near the Emuckfau battlefield the night before the battle, the line of march by Coffee's troops, including "friendly Creeks & Cherokees" noting where they forded the Tallapoosa River to encircle the bend. Unlike the other maps, Carroll illustrated spatial as well as temporal placement of the army. The disposition of the artillery as well as other units and their movement are given, along with their approximate position in yards at various points during the battle. The island itself is not shown, but a line of dots indicates the route taken by men dispatched there.

The map provides considerable detail on the movement of the allied Creek and Cherokee units, noting where the Cherokees crossed the river to procure canoes: "Cherokees crossed" and "Friendly Creeks crossed," each have a "covering party of whites." A notation indicates that the line of "outside dots [indicate] their Horses left under a guard the men formed in open order on the Bank of the River as represented by inside dots." The map does not indicate the location of the previously burned town of Nuyaka but deems the village inside the bend "New Yauca or Horse Shoe Town" indicated by a series of triangles. The map carries a scale of "200 yard to an Inch."

The remaining maps are largely unknown and, as far as can be determined, have never been utilized by historians or archaeologists studying Horseshoe Bend. Robert Houston McEwen (1790–1868), a relative of Sam Houston, was the regimental quartermaster for Colonel John Brown's Regiment of East Tennessee Militia. He enjoyed a successful career as a merchant in Tennessee after the war and later served as a school superintendent in Nashville. His map was retained by his wife, the sister of a fellow veteran of the battle, until her death. Although he drew his "description" of the battleground the morning after the battle, the information concerning the details of his military service is in different ink and was added "years after the battle" according to his descendant, who donated the map to the Library of Congress. Altogether, McEwen signed his map three times, with each additional annotation.[32]

FIGURE 13 (*opposite*). R. H. McEwen's map of the Battle of Horseshoe Bend. Courtesy of the Library of Congress, Geography and Map Division.

McEwen's map is notable for the personal details he added to the drawing, notably when and how he drew his map. Also important is the marked "sally part." The map includes three handwritten amendments, all of which McEwen signed:

Left side:
Being Quarter Master to a Regiment I was entitled to Carry a Sword, This I scorned to do as I went to fight, I therefore carried a large rifle the whole route.

Right side:
I drew This description of the battle ground & made the memorandums, on my hat the morning after the battle, the battle commenced about 10 Oclock A.M. & ended about sun down. I Was Regimental Quarter Master, to a regiment of six months Volunteers from East Tennessee Commanded By Col John Brown. we left Kinston, E. Ten. the 23d Jany 1814 for the Creek nation & returned to Kingston the 9 May 1814—the war With the Indians Being at an end. My Col being sick I had A high Command on the day of Battle.

Bottom:
This Battle fought on Sunday the 27th March 1814 557 enemy counted Dead on the ground, 25 of our men fell. 106 wounded some mortally—Its supposed numbers more of the enemy fell, but was draged into the river & not found.

The key appears at the bottom of the map, above McEwen's three annotations:

FIGURE 1 Represents the Breast Works

FIGURE 2 the Sally port which was a small avinue through which a man could just pass

The line marked thus . . . ++ represents the 39th Regt. Militia and Artillery charging the Works.

eeeee This Represents the Mounted Gun men on the opposite side of the river from the foot.

Being Quarter Master to a Regiment I was not entitled to carry a sword; this I wanted to, & I went to fight, I therefore carried a large rifle the whole route,

R.H. McEwen

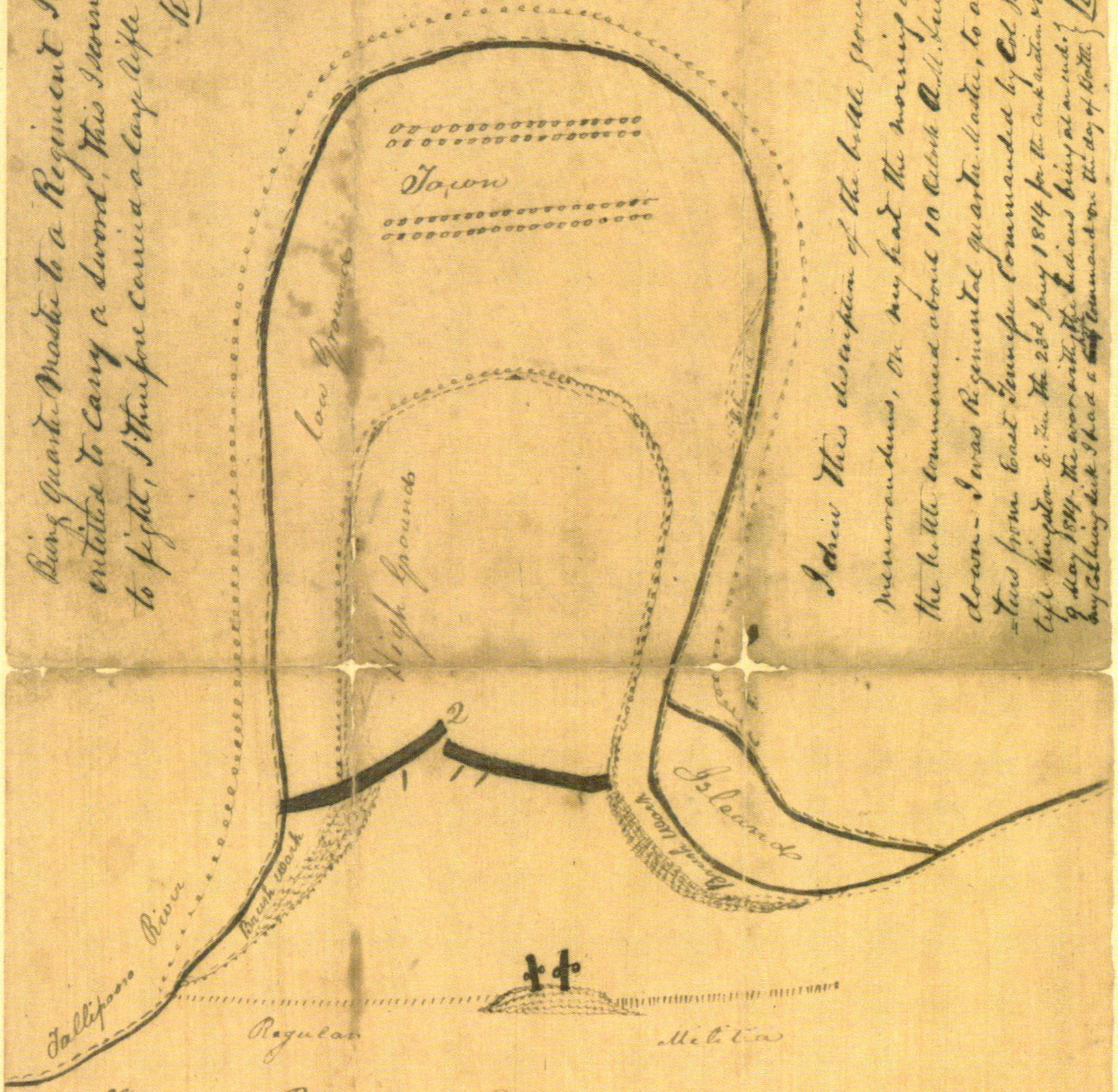

Town

Low Grounds

High Grounds

2

1

Island

Brush work

Tallapoosa River

Regular

Militia

I drew this description of the battle ground [illegible] the memorandums, on my hat the morning after the battle, the battle commenced about 10 o'clock A.M. ended about sun down — I was Regimental quarter Master to a regiment of [illegible] men from East Tennessee commanded by Col. John Brown. we left Kingston E. Ten. the 23d Jany 1814 for the Creek nation & returned to Kingston the [illegible] day of May 1814, [illegible]

R.H. McEwen

Figure 1 Represents the Breast Works

Figure 2 the Sally port which was a small avinue through which a man could just pass

The line marked thus [illegible] represents the 39th Regt Militia and Artillery Charging the Works

eeeee This Represents the Mounted Gun men on the opposite side of the river from the fort.

R.H. McEwen

This Battle fought on Sunday the 27th March 1814 557 enemy counted Dead on the ground. 25 of our men fell. 106 wounded some Mortally —

Its supposed numbers more of the enemy fell, but was [illegible] into the river & not found

The Tennessee State Library and Archives holds a photocopy of a manuscript map of unknown provenance titled *The Battle of Tahopta Fought the 27th of March 1814*. The map's cartographer, date, current location, and owner are unknown. But like the other small manuscript maps, this unsigned diagram was folded and likely sent home by a member of Jackson's army shortly after the battle.[33]

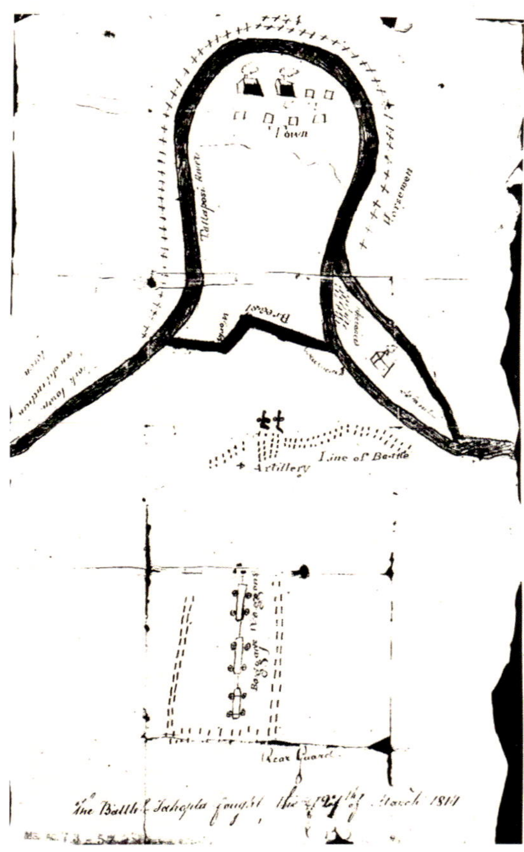

FIGURE 14. "The Battle of Tahopta fought the 27th of March 1814," a photocopy of the manuscript map, current location unknown. Courtesy of the Tennessee State Library and Archives, Photography Collection, AC. No. 72–57.

The sparse map is notable for a number of features. Specifically, the placement of a house symbol on the island and the unlabeled marking on the far western side of the barricade that perhaps was meant to indicate the covered ravine.

Isaac Stephens produced "A Correct View of the Battle of the Horse-Shoe" for his uncle Henry Mackey of Lexington, Virginia. The carefully constructed map, notable for its use of houses rather than tents or teepees to represent Indian habitations, indicated "300 Houses" at the battle, a far greater number than other sources. Stephens spent considerably more time drawing his plan than producing the one-paragraph letter it accompanied. In both documents, he remarked on the "unequalled bravery of the gallant Sons of Tennessee, commanded by General Jackson." His letter was posted from Blountville, Tennessee, on May 12, 1814, after his discharge.[34] After the war, Stephens established a farm and was the first representative from Bledsoe County, Tennessee, to serve in the Tennessee General Assembly.[35]

FIGURE 15 (*opposite*). "A Correct View of the Battle of the Horse-Shoe, March 27th 1814." Map drawn by Isaac Stephens. Courtesy of the Gilder Lehrman Institute of American History, GLC06772.

Stephens's map contains an artistic cartouche lauding the brave and patriotic American troops while noting the Creeks were "totally destroyed by the unequalled bravery of the gallant Sons of Tennessee, commanded by General Jackson." Stephens also indicated a sally port in the barricade as well as "Logs" on both the east and west sides of the "Works." His map provides important information missing from other sources—namely, that the island (now Bean's Island) "was fixed for cultivation" and that "300 Houses" were in the toe of the bend, indicated by a variety of house symbols.

The map's key is placed opposite the cartouche title and reads as follows:

References.

A. The Indian Town.
B. The Indian Breast Works.
C. An Island fixed for cultivation.
D. The Forces_Consisting of the 39th Regt. U. S. Infantry & two Brigades of Militia.
E. The American Encampment.
F. The Road & Crossings of the Cavalry and Cherokees.
G. The Contents of the Horse-Shoe, from 80 to 100 Acres.

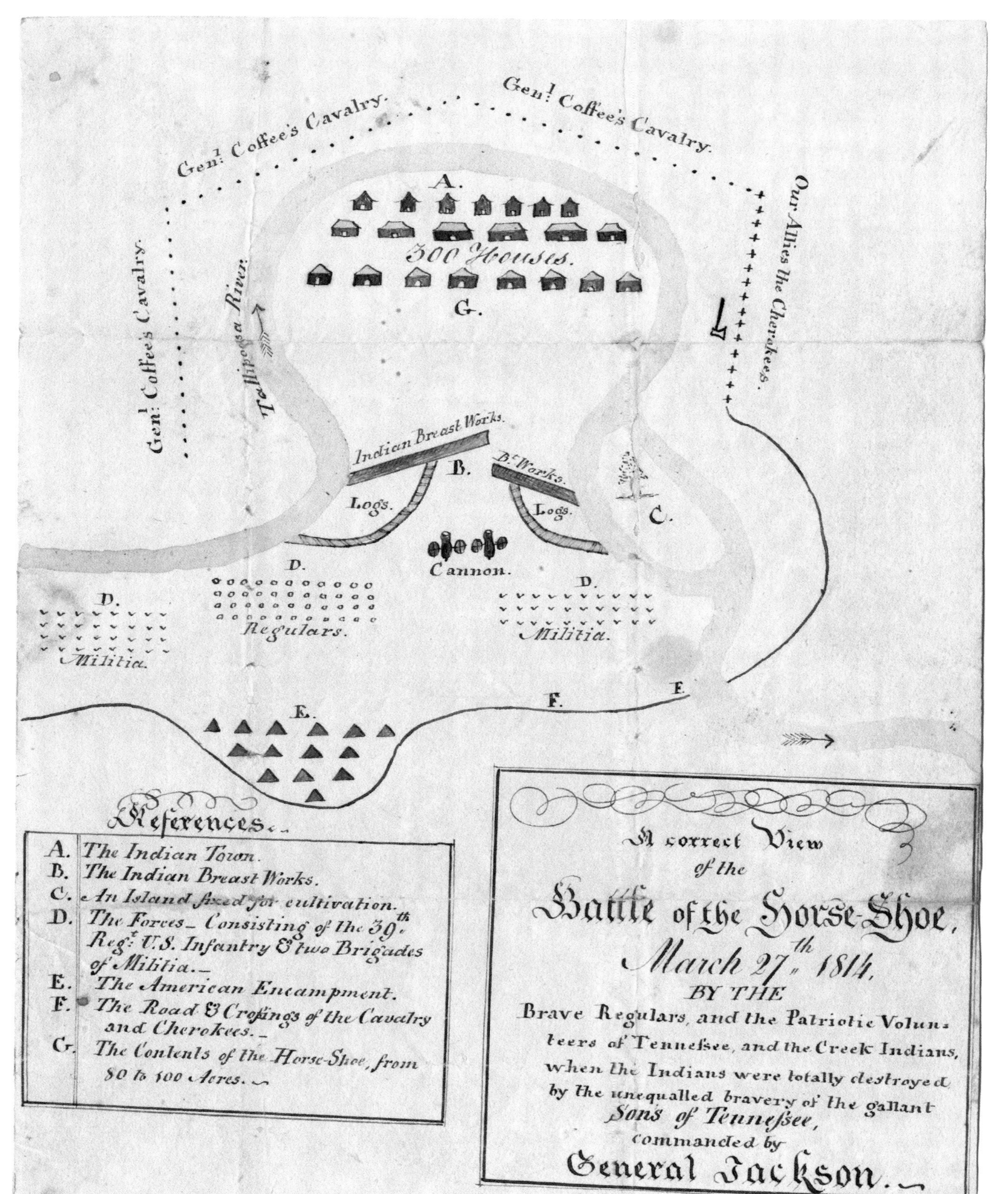

Genl. Coffee's Cavalry.
Genl. Coffee's Cavalry.
Genl. Coffee's Cavalry.
Our Allies the Cherokees.
A.
300 Houses.
G.
Tallipoosa River.
Indian Breast Works.
B.
Br. Works.
Logs.
Logs.
C.
Cannon.
D.
D.
D.
Regulars.
Militia.
Militia.
E.
F.
F.
References.
A. The Indian Town.
B. The Indian Breast Works.
C. An Island fixed for cultivation.
D. The Forces – Consisting of the 39th Regt. U.S. Infantry & two Brigades of Militia.
E. The American Encampment.
F. The Road & Crossings of the Cavalry and Cherokees.
G. The Contents of the Horse-Shoe, from 80 to 100 Acres.
A correct View of the Battle of the Horse-Shoe, March 27th 1814, BY THE Brave Regulars, and the Patriotic Volunteers of Tennessee, and the Creek Indians, when the Indians were totally destroyed by the unequalled bravery of the gallant Sons of Tennessee, commanded by General Jackson.

Another map, with the caption torn but otherwise intact, resides in the Library of Congress. Cataloged as "Battle of Tehoo[pca]," the map's reverse carries what appears to be the contemporary title *Plan of Bend and Breast Works of Tohopeka the Battle of the 27th March 1814*.[36]

FIGURE 16 (*opposite*). Sketch of "Battle of Tehoo[pca]" by unknown soldier. Courtesy of the Library of Congress, Geography and Map Division.

The small map's title is partially missing due to the torn upper-right corner. The drawing shows the initial positions of various components of the American army as well as the "March of the Infantry" from the campsite on the 26th to the battlefield. Likewise, the disposition of Coffee's troops including their return through the previously burned village of Nuyaka is indicated. The barricade is depicted as a complex series of angles to the east and a straight line approaching the western side of the bend.

The key reads as follows:

– – – The Cheerokees

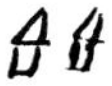

Indian villages

Battleground of Emuchfaw

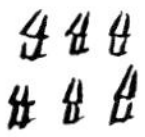

Encampment saturday 6 miles from Tehoopcan

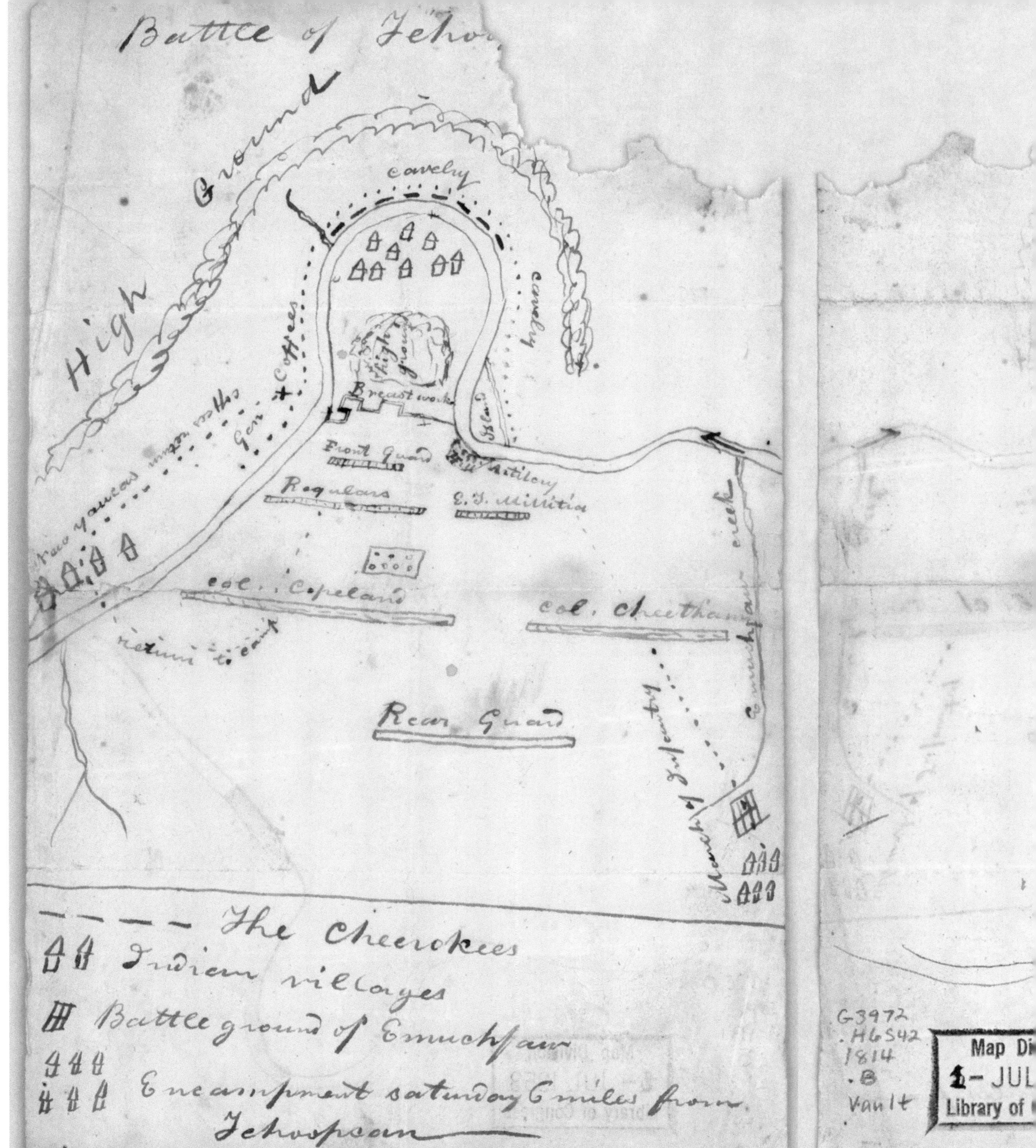

Battle of Teho
High Ground
cavelry
cavelry
Gen. Coffees
Breast work
Island
Front Guard
Artilery
Regulars
E. T. Militia
col. Copeland
col. Cheetham
return to camp
Rear Guard
March of Infantry
Emuchfaw creek
The Cheerokees
Indian villages
Battle ground of Emuchfaw
Encampment saturday 6 miles from Tehoopeau

The University of Tennessee Libraries holds another map of uncertain provenance. It was originally cataloged by the address on the map: Rhea County. The map bears the date May 15, 1814, which appears to be the date it was mailed.[37] In addition to these private and official manuscript maps, printed reproductions based on them as well as others soon appeared as prints and book illustrations.

FIGURE 17. Hand-drawn map of the Horseshoe Bend battleground mailed to Rhea County, Tennessee. Courtesy of the University of Tennessee Libraries, Knoxville, Betsey B. Creekmore Special Collections and University Archives, Map regarding the Battle of Horseshoe Bend, MS.0352.

The map is boldly rendered in red and black ink. The tattered map by an anonymous cartographer is marred by doodling added later by an unknown hand. Collaboration or at least common understanding between this mapmaker and Holmes, who produced the map for Leonard Tarrant, is indicated by the use of similar wording, particularly the unusual remark "second Bank of the River" for the high ground on the peninsula. Like the Tarrant map, the "Mountain" where Coffee oversaw his forces, "Coffee's Stand," as well as "A Craggy chain of hills," is noted. A significant annotation indicates that Coffee's "Brigade of horses crossed the River 2½ miles Below the Island." The site where the Cherokees "crossed the River" is obscured by stains and a tear. As in the map by Robert McEwen, this production shows a sally port. Red hash marks, representing the Red Stick Creeks, populate the barricade and are scattered both in the high ground and low land near the river. The notation "Red sicks Running" is repeated along both the east and west sides of the bend.

Brigade

The quality of these maps varies greatly. Lieutenant McEwen's was not a work of high cartographic art but rather a hastily done line sketch on a little piece of notepaper. McEwen used the top of his hat as his drawing surface.[38] Others, like the presentation map later produced by J. L. Holmes for Captain Leonard L. Tarrant, show not only greater detail but also color and intrinsic artistry.[39] All are pen and ink, with occasional use of blue or red coloration.

All the currently identified maps reproduce the defining topographical and built features of the battleground: the massive horseshoe bend of the Tallapoosa River and the formidable breastwork protecting the peninsula. These two key elements merged into a unified scene in the mind of both Jackson and his men. Jackson himself noted, "As a situation for defense it was selected with judgement, and improved with great industry and art."[40] In Jackson's words:

> This bend resembles, in its curvature that of a horse-shoe, & is thence called by that name among the whites. Nature furnishes few situations so eligible for defense; & barbarians have never rendered one more secure by art. Across the neck of land which leads into it from the North, they had erected a breast-work, of greatest compactness & strength—from five to eight feet high, & prepared with double rows of port-holes very artfully arranged. The figure of this wall, manifested no less skill in the projectors of it, than its construction: an army could not approach it without being exposed to a double and cross fire from the enemy who lay in perfect security behind it. The area of this peninsular, thus bounded by the breast-work includes, I conjecture eighty or a hundred acres.[41]

All the maps include the terrain features that figured prominently in the battle, including the island that lies on the west side of the river, where Lieutenant Jesse Bean's Company of Mounted Spies was ensconced; the hill on which Jackson deployed his artillery, some eighty yards from the Creek fortification; the "high ground" of pine ridges that mirrored the curvature of the river bend; and "broken ground" and other important sites, such as the site of the previously destroyed Creek town of Nuyaka and the newly constructed Indian town in the bend of the river. A variety of conventions, including captions, show the American army's placement and troop deployments, notably General John Coffee's movement to encircle the river bend (to prevent the escape of Red Sticks and prevent reinforcement from the rear), the location of the Creek and Cherokees fighting with the American army, and the manner in which Jackson's other forces, including artillery, militia, and regulars, were stationed and moved through the course of the battle. The landscape itself and the manner in which the American military prevailed are highlighted by the cartographers. Landscape features not closely associated with the battle, such as cane breaks and springs, are largely absent. The maps, in effect, tell the stories of the operations that in the eyes of his officers made Jackson a national hero and filled them with pride in their achievement. And this was indeed their purpose.

Scholars, of course, look to the maps for clues about the battle, some believing that the documents are attempts at capturing geographic realities. The maps are valuable productions for their evidentiary value alone, providing interesting and informative pictorial representations of the battle—its terrain, troop movements, and various components of the engagement. But the number of maps produced by veterans of the battle at the Horseshoe stands in marked contrast to the lack of battle maps for other actions and suggests something more than enthusiasm for geographic elucidation and an attempt to accurately replicate spatial information.

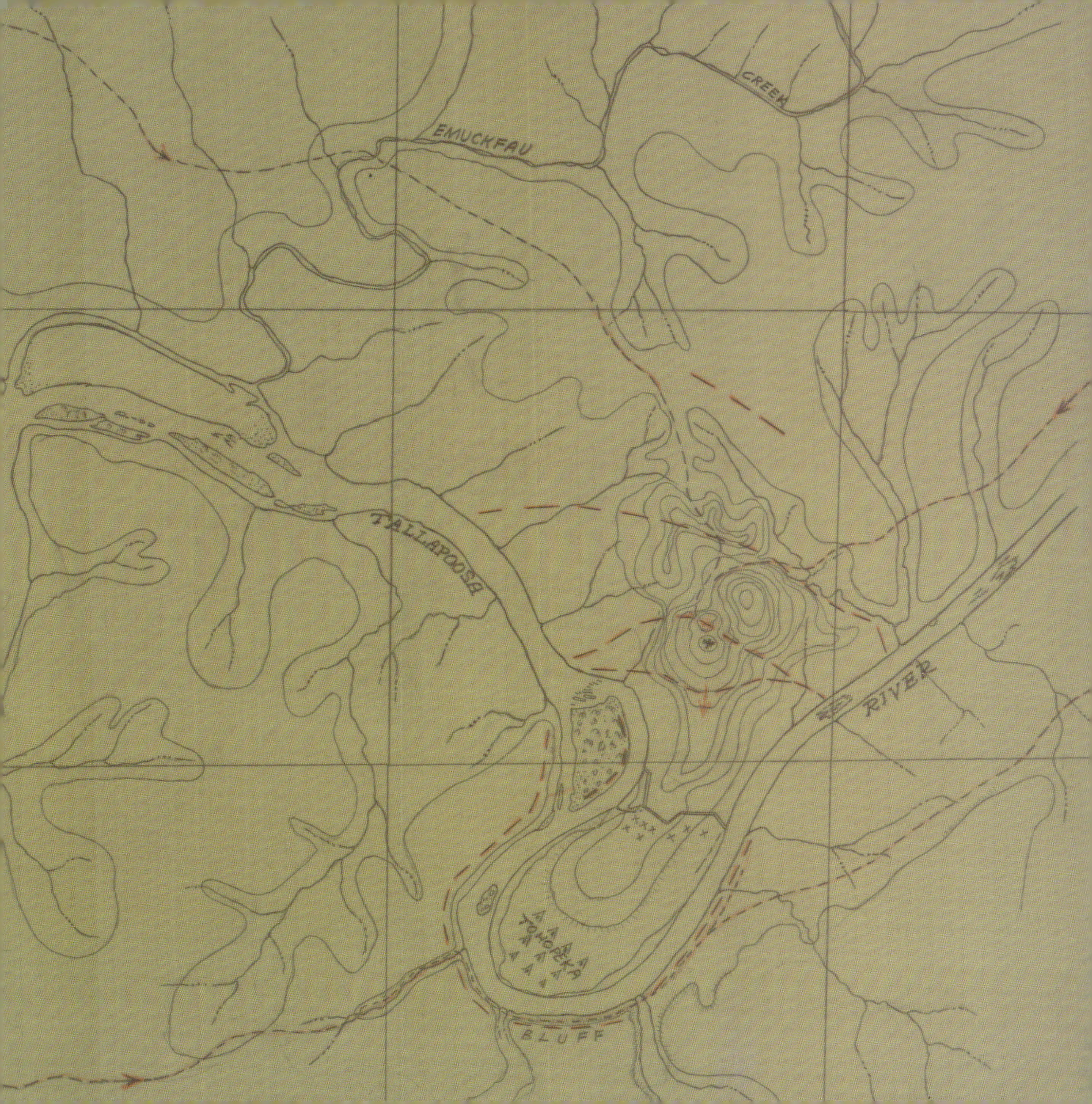
EMUCKFAU
CREEK
TALLAPOOSA
RIVER
TOHOPEKA
BLUFF

CHAPTER 2

The Barricade

The most important element of the battle—and the subject of intense scholarly scrutiny—is the exact location and design of the barricade constructed by the Red Sticks. All the maps portray it but with varying inexactitude that has stumped scholars as much as the barricade itself impeded Jackson's forces. The fortification as described by William Carroll was "composed of large logs laid one above the other from 5 to 8 feet high."[1]

The stout structure embraced the elevation of the terrain and proved a strong fortress. Chief engineer Bradford's two artillery pieces did "not make a breach in it." As the seasoned military engineer observed, "It was built with all the military skills the ground would afford—."[2] The result was that after two hours of ineffective cannon fire with grapeshot, the Americans had managed to kill some Red Sticks behind their barricade, but return rifle fire from the barricade had inflicted casualties on the American artillery crew and made a direct frontal assault a deadly proposition.[3]

Across the peninsula, the Cherokees under John Coffee's command launched an unplanned and unauthorized operation. Led by Private The Whale, three Cherokees swam the cold Tallapoosa, secured canoes lining the opposite bank to ferry Creek and Cherokee warriors into the village, where they set fire to the houses and began fighting their way up the peninsula.[4] The resulting confusion, and need to protect their rear, diverted Red Sticks from their advance positions. At that point, the Americans saw their opportunity and stormed the barricade.

The Americans sustained most of their casualties at the breastwork, where those clambering toward and over the log wall made easy targets for the defenders. Coffee, in charge of the army's Cherokee and Creek units, reported that "it was not unusual for the muzzles of the guns of both parties to meet in the port holes and both fire at the same time."[5] As Andrew Jackson and John Reid confirmed, "the balls of the enemy were found welded to the muzzles of our guns."[6]

Once the Americans made it over the breastwork, they found themselves in fierce hand-to-hand combat in what Major Reid described as a "contest . . . not so much for victory as for life."[7] Defenders were armed with muskets or rifles as well as war clubs and scalping knives. The defenders were also protected with what one wounded American deemed "a ditch covered with brush." Red Sticks fired at their frontal attackers from these protected positions and, via these same entrenchments, initially held off the Cherokees, who took the high ground behind the barricade but could not dislodge the Red Sticks.[8] Colonel Gideon Morgan [Jr.], who commanded the Cherokees, noted "the declivity & flat which surrounded it [the 'high ground' behind the barricade] was filled with fallen timber, the growth of which was very heavy, and had been so arranged that every tree afforded them a breast work, forming a communication or cover to the next, and so on to the river bank, in which caverns had been dug for their security, and our annoyance."[9] Encircled and outnumbered, the Red Sticks would not

FIGURE 18. Presentation rifle designated but never delivered to The Whale. The rifle is embellished with solid silver ornaments. The engraving on the patch box reads "Presented by J. Madison, President of the U.S. To Whale the Reward of Signal Valor & Heroism; at the Battle of the Horse-Shoe. March, 1814." The rifle is part of the collection of Horseshoe Bend National Military Park. Photo courtesy of Horseshoe Bend National Military Park, National Park Service.

surrender and fought to escape or die honorably in battle. Sam Houston, who served with the Thirty-Ninth Regiment, recalled years later, "Not a warrior offered to surrender, even while the sword was at his breast."[10] As Jackson would report, "It was dark before we finished killing them."[11]

Jackson ordered a count of the Red Stick dead on the battlefield, but the Americans made no efforts to bury the bodies and quickly left the battleground the next day to return to Fort Williams on the Coosa River. Jackson seemed to refer to the site in his farewell speech to the Tennessee troops, distributed April 28, 1814, at Fort Williams: "We have seen the ravens & the vultures preying upon the carcases of the . . . unburied slain."[12] After the Creek War, the battlefield remained Creek land for just over two decades until it was lost during the removal era; however, reports indicate the Creeks largely avoided the site of the horrific battle. The location of the battlefield was never in doubt, and once the land became American territory in 1832, early Alabamians celebrated the site of the military victory as a seminal step in the transformation of the land from Indian to American territory. At the beginning of the twentieth century, the remains of the barricade were still visible. Members of Alabama's Horseshoe Bend Battle Commission, appointed to commemorate the centennial of the battle, visited the site in 1907 and easily found "the location of the old breastworks, which in the long years has become quite a little ridge of earth, curving toward the center and grown up with trees, and extending a great part of the way across the neck of the bend."[13] Plowing, agricultural terracing, and other activities had eradicated the telltale ridge of the defensive works by the time efforts by private citizens, civic groups, and state organizations finally resulted in the establishment of the Horseshoe Bend National Military Park in 1965.[14]

It was not until the National Park Service (NPS) acquired the property that professional archaeologists began to study the site. The first investigations were carried out by Charles H. Fairbanks in 1961. Fairbanks's limited survey included attempts to locate the Tohopeka "village" in the toe of the bend and the Creek town of Nuyaka, part of which was located on NPS property, as well as the breastworks. Fairbanks recognized the importance of the barricade location to park interpretation but concentrated

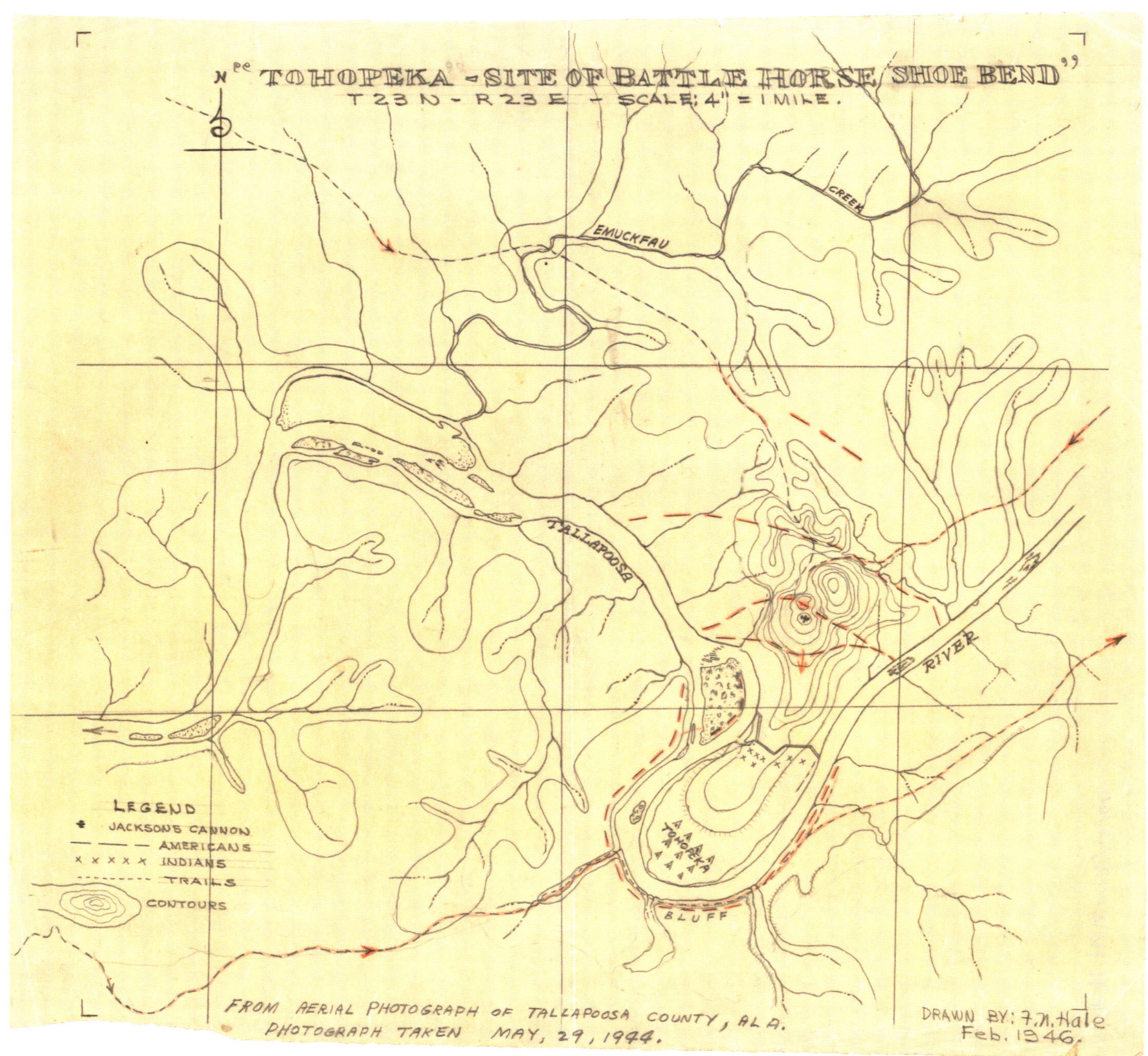

FIGURE 19. Fletcher Hale, a surveyor with an interest in Alabama history, was among the first to use aerial photography to study the battle. It is unclear why he depicted the barricade as he did. In 1944, remnants of the barricade were still obvious according to local witnesses, so it is possible he based his barricade line on visual evidence. Hale based his map on photographs done by the U.S. Department of Agriculture's Agricultural Adjustment Administration. Courtesy of the Alabama Department of Archives and History.

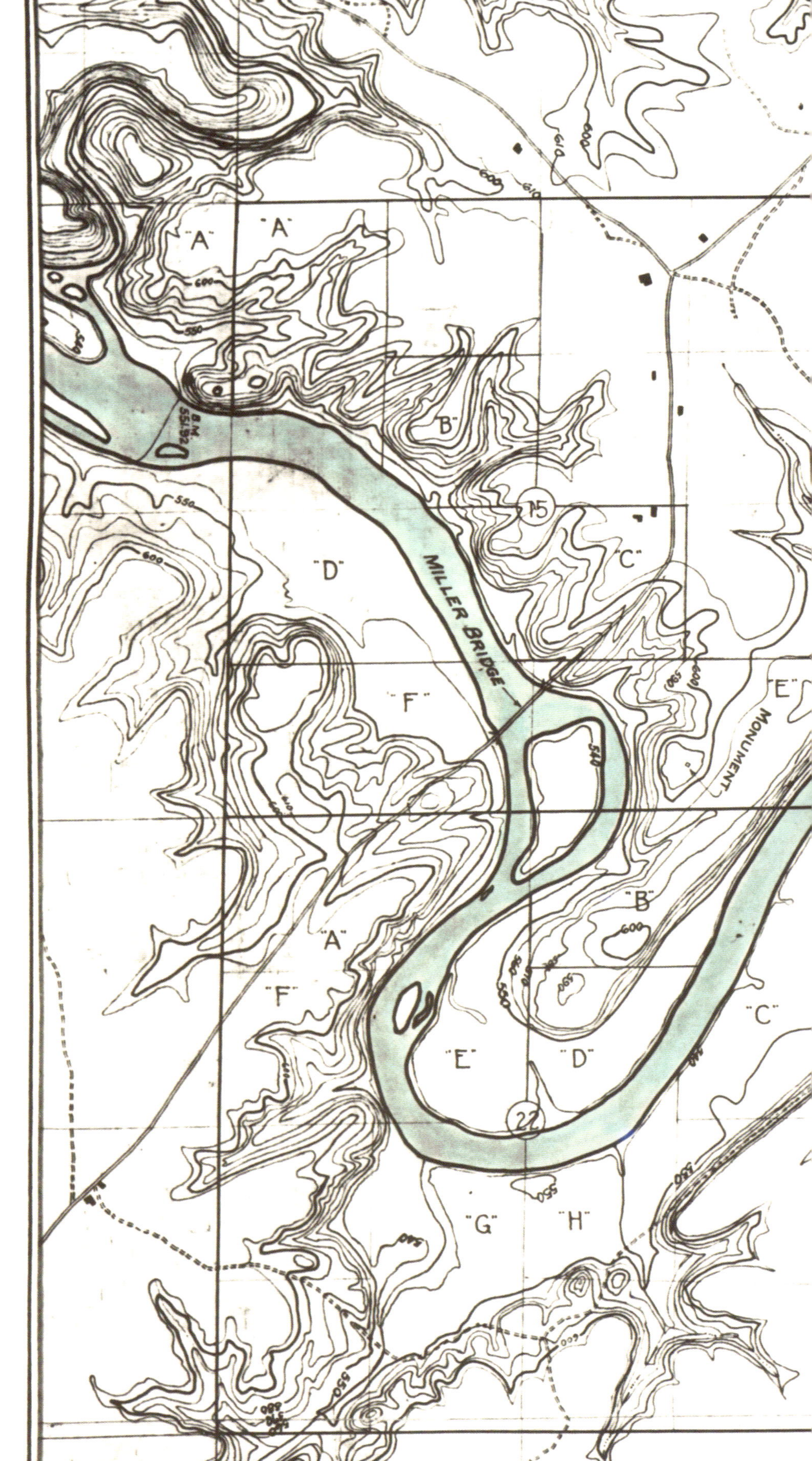

FIGURE 20. Map produced in 1956 as part of the effort to have the battle site declared a national military park. Local landowners as well as Alabama Power Company donated the property for the park's establishment. Courtesy of the Birmingham Public Library.

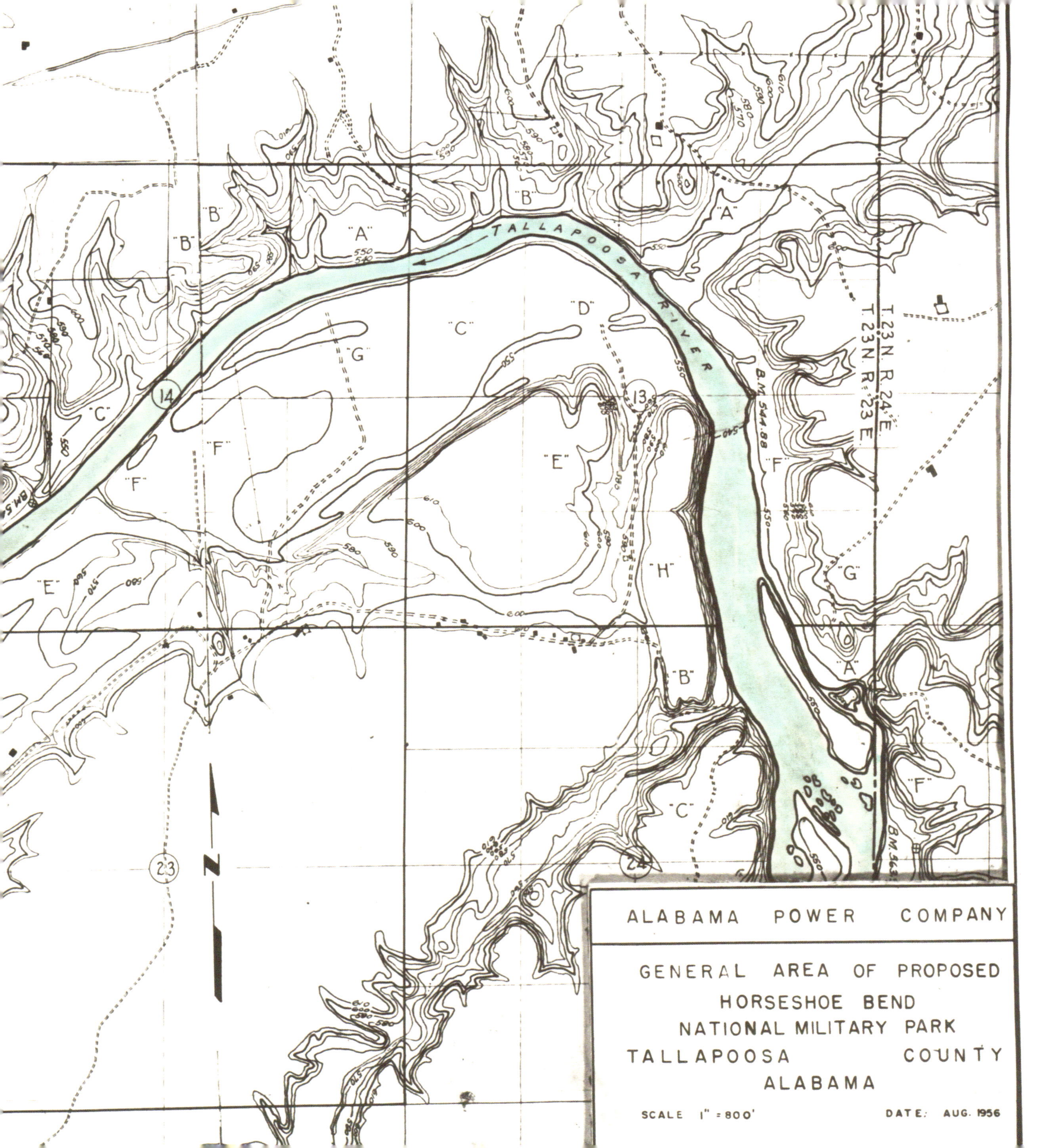

TALLAPOOSA RIVER
B.M. 544.88
T. 23 N. R. 24 E.
T. 23 N. R. 23 E.
ALABAMA POWER COMPANY
GENERAL AREA OF PROPOSED
HORSESHOE BEND
NATIONAL MILITARY PARK
TALLAPOOSA COUNTY
ALABAMA
SCALE 1" = 800'
DATE: AUG. 1956

on the village sites. His trenches on the battlefield yielded little data, and he concluded, "There now remains no possibility of locating the Indian fortifications."[15] This assertion temporarily halted further attempts to locate the structure until 1964, when construction of a road unearthed "discolored deposits" that appeared to park historian Glenn Hinsdale to be carbon—evidence of the burned barricade. Hinsdale, in a report to the NPS, sought to reopen archaeological investigations by pointing out the obvious flaws in Fairbanks's work. He noted the limited excavations carried out and condemned even that cursory effort by observing that the primary focus of Fairbanks's investigation had been the spot where Jackson's troops were deployed prior to the battle and later a soil conservation terrace.

Like Hinsdale, many local residents had never accepted Fairbanks's declaration of "futility" in finding the barricade. Jack Coley, a local attorney who had spearheaded the effort to have the site made a national military park, worked with Hinsdale to subvert Fairbanks's conclusion and found three "elderly eyewitnesses, who independently recollected the existence of distinct remains of what they had identified as at least a portion of the Indian fortification." Each of them in turn led Hinsdale to roughly the same location—away from Fairbanks's original trench sites. In addition to local knowledge and historical memory, Hinsdale relied heavily on the documentary record to overcome the strength of Fairbanks's published work, turning to battlefield reports and manuscript maps available to him. Hinsdale concluded that Fairbanks was "unquestionably accurate about the barricade not being present where he looked" and made a strong case for further testing to ascertain the actual location of the barricade. His methodology, stressing close attention to the documentary record, particularly the cartographic record, had a lasting impact on future archaeological efforts at the site.[16]

The immediate result of Hinsdale's efforts was a comprehensive study of the issue by NPS historian George C. Mackenzie. His work provided an overview of the site's history, including terracing work during the 1930s as part of an effort to halt erosion, timbering activity, and the impact of Alabama Power's construction of Martin Dam on the Tallapoosa River. He concluded that although "there have been some terrain changes at certain locations within the park, these do not appear to have been so extensive as to eliminate all traces of the breastwork remains, which are thought to be in areas relatively unspoiled by man or nature."[17] Mackenzie agreed with Hinsdale that Fairbanks had been north of the "historically determined" site of the barricade that park personnel had established based on their study of three manuscript maps of the battle.[18] Park interpretation of the barricade at that time consisted of a staggered line of eight-foot-tall white posts ranging across the neck of the bend. Mackenzie cogently observed, "To just view the posts, they do not even suggest a breastwork. The writer found this manner of identifying the site of the Indian breastwork most disappointing, and entirely inadequate from the standpoint of effective interpretation."[19]

Moreover, Mackenzie observed that while the posts were in the "general vicinity" of the estimated location of the barricade, it was likely to be "an estimated 30 feet south of the presently marked site." Noting that the breastwork "represents the most crucial element within the story of events associated with the Battle of Horseshoe Bend," he strongly encouraged further archaeological investigations to confirm or adjust the "historically determined site" since only archaeological evidence could resolve the mystery of the barricade's exact location. The ultimate goal of such research would be "a reconstruction of at least a portion of the original fortification."[20] In their research, both Hinsdale and Mackenzie used the map owned by the Tennessee Historical Society, which they believed had been drafted by Jackson, the Tarrant map that they inexplicably identified as "John Coffee's Map," and the Cheatham map owned by the National Archives and Records Administration. Mackenzie accepted without question that the "Andrew Jackson" map was the production of the general (as evidenced by the use of military symbols) but conceded that in regard to the Tohopeka village and breastwork, "it is believed the manner in which they are drawn is thus only intended to be representative." He likewise deemed the Tarrant map (misidentified as John Coffee's map) as "a rough sketch . . . as one would expect a layman to draw," seemingly unaware that Coffee was a surveyor. He declared the Cheatham map "easily the best map of the three" and thought it presented "the greatest possibility of accuracy" in regard to

FIGURE 21. Interpretative diorama of the assault on the barricade by the Thirty-Ninth U.S. Regiment, a popular feature of the museum at Horseshoe Bend National Military Park from 1964 to 2020. Photo courtesy of the author.

location of the barricade given that the configuration depicted would have allowed for the deadly cross fire encountered by the attackers.[21] In his own report, completed in 1969, Mackenzie annotated a copy of a map produced by Hinsdale to locate the "historically determined site" of the barricade to include the "projected" outline of Cheatham's barricade line.[22] The report concluded with observations on Red Stick construction methods, with a "highly conjectural" attempt at describing what the barricade would have looked like. Mackenzie favored a series of "staggered posts put down in the ground at regularly spaced intervals with logs laid one up on the other set down between these supporting members." As he observed, "To erect a breastwork in this manner would have been relatively simple, and it could have been accomplished without the expenditure of an excessive amount of time." He observed that this proposed design failed to account for clay fill, which he noted was "mentioned as having been present in some accounts." To address that issue, he included a "highly conjectural" diagram of dual wall construction that included clay fill.[23]

The notion of double-wall construction with clay fill seems to have been based on a line from James Parton's *Life of Andrew Jackson* (1861). According to this secondary account, "The little cannon balls buried themselves in the logs, or in the earth between them, without doing decisive harm."[24] Yet no extant battlefield letter or report mentions clay fill or chinking between the logs of the breastwork. Instead, Jackson wrote to his wife that his cannonballs "passed thro the works without shaking the wall."[25] John Reid reported the same: "Our balls only passed through [the barricade], killing some behind it, but doing no material injury to the works." Reid also remarked that the artillery, loaded with antipersonnel grapeshot, purposefully aimed at any Red Sticks coming from the village to reinforce the barricade and reported, "We kept up a brisk fire up in such of the enemy as shewed themselves behind the wall or endeavored to approach it from the town, which was situated at the lower extremity of the peninsula." Meanwhile, as Reid and others reported, the Red Sticks fired at the Americans through their "portholes." This letter by Reid to his wife has also been used to support the notion of a double-walled construction. But Reid's observation that "the enemy were very well defended by logs on the inner side also" likely referred to secondary fallback or part of a log-reinforced trench behind the barricade rather than a double-wall construction.[26]

In 1973, the NPS contracted with Dr. Roy S. Dickens Jr. to renew archaeological investigations at the "village" in the toe of the bend and the barricade. Dickens and his team employed a variety of techniques including soil resistivity testing, metal detecting, and trenching. Prior to the actual work, Dickens embarked on an aerial reconnaissance of the site and used aerial photographs, alongside historic maps, in an attempt to narrow the search area for the barricade. Given the desire of park personnel to reconstruct the barricade for interpretative purposes, Dickens was particularly attuned to any evidence that might suggest structural details. Three manuscript maps played a large role in determining the location of his trenches. Like Hinsdale, Dickens attempted to plot the location of the barricade using the same three maps. His trencher excavations located "a footing ditch, borrow pits, burned debris, and a patterned distribution of ammunition from the battle." His analysis of the five grader trenches, roughly twelve feet wide and designed to bisect the barricade area, led him to surmise that "the barricade appears to have been constructed of two parallel rows of horizonal logs, with the lower tiers set in a shallow ditch. Clay was packed in the space between the two walls, and vertical posts provided support on either side of the earth-and-log structure." Although he concluded that this reconstruction corresponded to Cheatham's rendering of the wall, his improbable interpretation of the features he located resulted in a structure that in no way matched historical accounts, Creek construction practices, or practical considerations faced by the builders.[27] Nonetheless, his hypothetical rendering of the Creek barricade was used for interpretative purposes at the park. As archaeologist Gregory A. Waselkov noted in a 1986 essay on the barricade, the conjectural reconstructions of Mackenzie and Dickens were "very probably not feasible" in addition to ignoring historical evidence and traditional Creek building practices.[28]

Further investigations in 2006 by John Cornelison of the Southeast Archeological Center (SEAC) sought to use metal detector technology, which had seen significant advances since earlier fieldwork, to further pin down the barricade's location. Based on Jackson's use of artillery against the barricade for two hours, the investigators assumed that large numbers of impacted rounds could be recovered from the front of the barricade while a different pattern would be revealed behind the barricade—ignoring that fire had been aimed at men behind the barricade. As they ultimately noted, "unfortunately, this pattern did not manifest in a manner that was easily discernible."[29] Cornelison's team also relied heavily on historical maps to pinpoint the location for their metal survey. Using the same maps employed by McKenzie (the "Jackson" map, Tarrant map, and Cheatham map), the team used a Map-O-Graph machine to enlarge the small manuscript maps to the scale of modern maps and used geographic information system (GIS) techniques to "rectify" the hand-drawn maps to fit current topographical features. To account for the obvious errors in the original maps, like Dickens, Cornelison used topographical features to scale the original maps and test their accuracy. However, the locations shown by the rectified maps proved problematic when compared to the known distance of Gun Hill from the barricade.[30] Although they did recover 328 objects, including both fired and unfired bullets, canister and grapeshot, and other bits of metal, the work ultimately shed little light on the location of the barricade line or the manner of the structure's construction. The most substantial result of the work was that the distribution of artifacts, when duly plotted, led them to question Dickens's interpretation of the barricade's location.

The use of selected historical maps—stretched and contorted to conform to the actual landscape—were also an essential component in planning for the latest (2017) archaeological effort. Using maps and some evidence gleaned from letters and military reports, the SEAC team, again led by Cornelison, scanned the same three manuscript maps into a GIS program and, once again, "electronically rectified" the manuscript maps to the current landscape. Using these data, the team suggested modifications to the suspected barricade line, which differed from both that used by the park for interpretation as well as the line suggested by Dickens earlier. The subsequent investigation

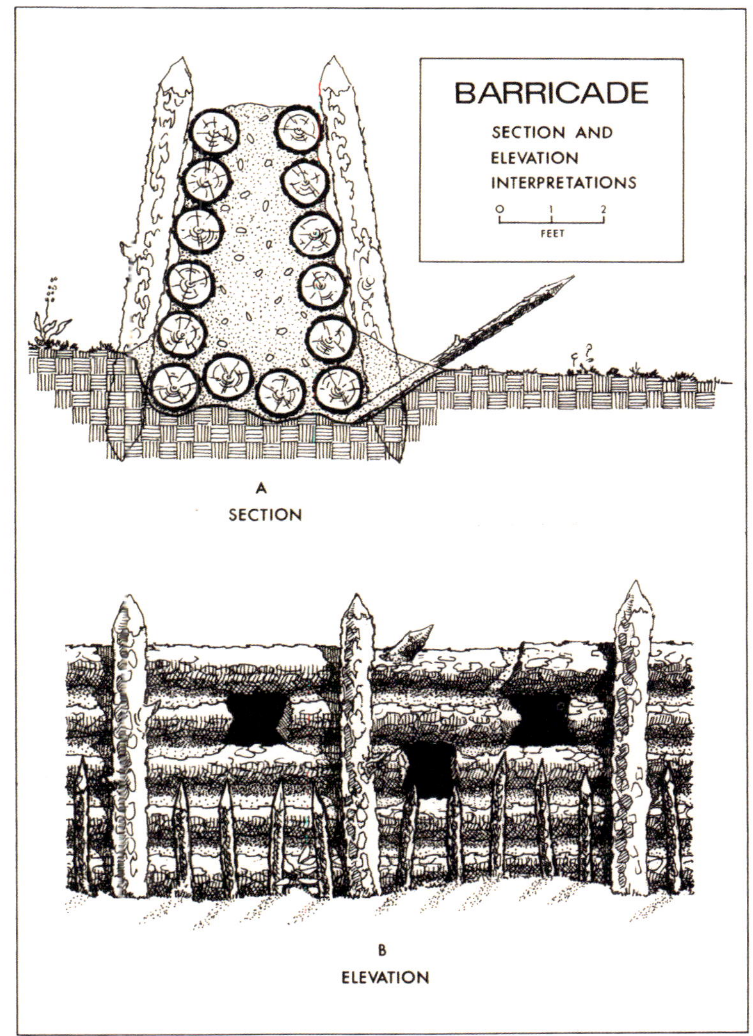

FIGURE 22. Conjectural "Section and Elevation Interpretations of the Barricade," figure 33 from Roy S. Dickens Jr., *Archaeological Investigations at Horseshoe Bend National Military Park, Alabama*, Special Publications of the Alabama Archaeological Society, Number 3, December 1979.

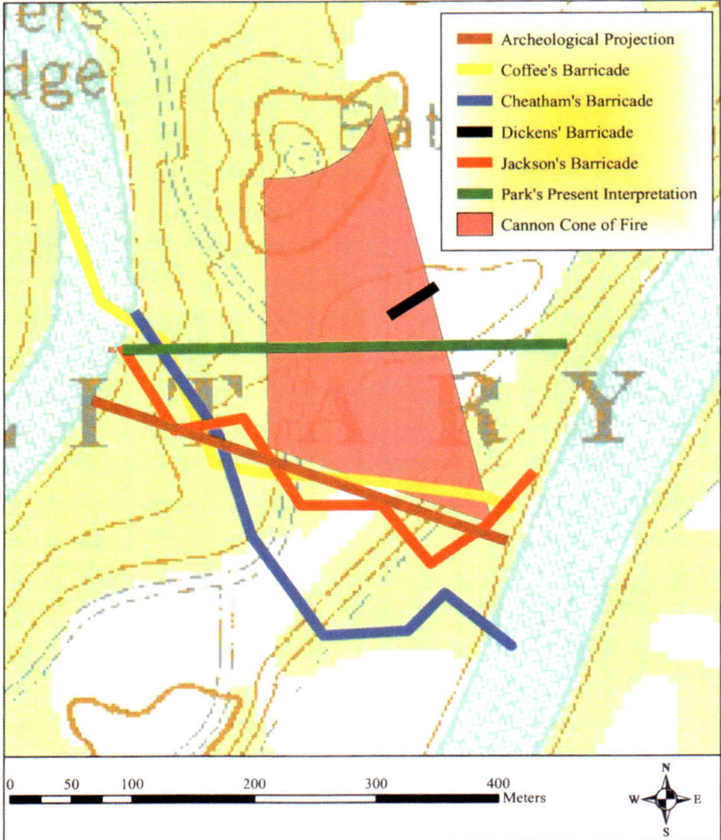

FIGURE 23. Diagram produced by John Cornelison's team illustrating the position of the barricade from the historic maps and the park's interpretation. From Cornelison's *Barricade* report. Courtesy of the Horseshoe Bend National Military Park, National Park Service.

employed a variety of enhanced archaeological techniques, including ground penetrating radar (GPR) as well as soil resistivity, conductivity, and gradiometer. The magnetic gradiometer and resistivity units, according to the investigators, "both clearly showed the archeological remains of the barricade."[31]

Cornelison's team wrote confidently that "based on the metal detecting and geophysical surveys, it is clear that the barricade was located along the slope facing Gun Hill. The palisade followed the contours of the slope, running southwest to northeast . . . and was not located on the topographic crest but what would be considered the military crest." The report noted such a "location offered protection from incoming projectiles, but also allowed the Creeks a strategic height advantage over incoming attackers, even in retreat." Cornelison's team abandoned the double-wall construction hypothesis, accepting Waselkov's conclusions and alternate reconstruction.[32]

Ironically, the team concluded that the map attributed to Andrew Jackson appeared to be "the most accurate" of the historical maps based on their rectification, particularly "in the shape and orientation of the bend, island, and villages." At the same time, they noted that the Jackson map placed Gun Hill too close to the Tallapoosa River and incorrectly rendered the western bank of the river. The Cheatham map—the only extant map known to have been drawn to scale in regard to the river bend and barricade—was deemed likely to be the most accurate depiction of the barricade itself, which they described as "an inverted redan . . . consistent with eyewitness accounts that describe Jackson's troops facing enfilading fire as they approached the barricade."[33]

The various archaeological investigations, employing a variety of increasingly sophisticated technologies, have made important finds in regard to the location of the barricade. But reliance on a limited selection of manuscript maps, selected documents, and early secondary sources devoid of substantial documentation has handicapped efforts to interpret the barricade.

The manuscript maps, many never previously identified or considered, add new layers of complexity to the puzzle of the "Indian Breast Works" layout and construction. The maps by Isaac Stephens and Robert McEwen clearly show a break

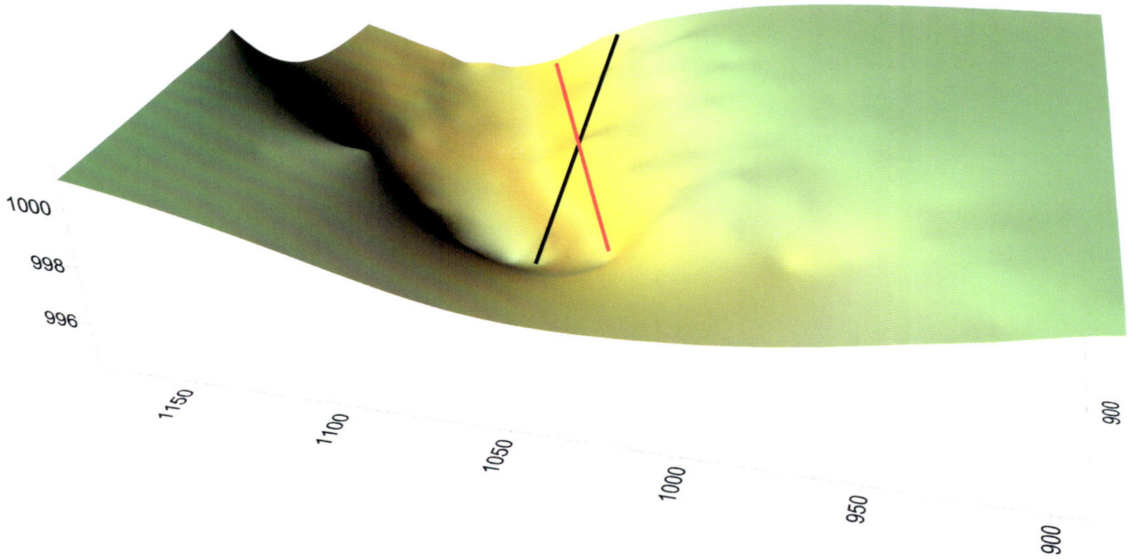

FIGURE 24. Topographic map produced by Cornelison's team indicating the line of the park's interpretative posts (black line) and the proposed location of the barricade based on remote sensing (red line). The red line, as noted by Cornelison's report, "follows the contours of the landscape, providing the strongest possible barrier to attack." Cornelison's 2018 report on the barricade, on file at Horseshoe Bend National Military Park, p. 71. Courtesy of Horseshoe Bend National Military Park, National Park Service.

in the barricade. The map by an unnamed soldier mailed to Rhea County, Tennessee, likewise shows the central break in the nearly quarter-mile-long barricade. McEwen highlighted the sally port in his legend and noted it "was a small avinue through which a man could just pass." None of the extant accounts of the battle mention the sally port, making McEwen's observation all the more significant.[34] The characteristic zigzag pattern of the barricade's angles in the map generally attributed to Andrew Jackson is repeated in the map produced by Colonel Carroll. John Reid referred to the "zig zag form of the wall" in a letter to his father.[35] The Carroll map supplies new insights, depicting a series of zigzags (likely brush impediments) in front of an angled wall similar to a number of other maps.

Another important detail appearing on several of the manuscript maps has been overlooked in attempts to fully conceive the fortification. Isaac Stephens, in his "A Correct View of the Battle of the Horse-Shoe," depicted two curved arcs, labeled "Logs" outside the "Indian Breast Works." The "Battle of Tahopka" by an unidentified hand likewise illustrates a rough arched element in the low ground outside the "Breast Work." Although uncaptioned, it clearly seems to represent a structure or impediment of some sort outside the main fortification. Robert McEwen's map also indicated "Brush Work" on both sides of the barricade.

The engraved map that accompanied Charles E. Lester's *The Life of Sam Houston*, published in 1866, along with Lester's written account of Sam Houston's participation in the battle, provides more detail about this element of the fortification. The map labels the "Covered Ravine" where Sam Houston was wounded as he "dashed down the precipitous descent, towards the covered ravine," where "a large party of Indians had secreted themselves in a part of the breastworks, constructed over a ravine in the form of the roof of a house, with narrow port-holes, from which a murderous fire could be kept up, whenever the assailants should show themselves."[36] Andrew Jackson, accompanied by his interpreter, George Mayfield, ventured within thirty paces of this structure and, while taking cover behind a nearby black oak tree, attempted to convince the Red Stick Creeks ensconced there to surrender since they were penned down and cut off from escape. The Red Sticks fired on Jackson and Mayfield, narrowly missing Jackson and wounding Mayfield. The defenders were ultimately killed when the Americans set the "brushworks" on fire.[37] This engraved map, likely derived from a manuscript map produced soon after the battle, clearly indicates the ravine or low area between the log barricade and the river.

Gideon Morgan, in his description of the barricade, noted that the "high ground which extended about mid-way from the breast work to the river was in some manner open, but the declivity & flat which surrounded it was filled with fallen timber, the growth of which was very heavy, and had been so arranged that every tree afforded them a breast work, forming a communication or cover to the next, and so on to the river bank, in which caverns had been dug for their security, and our annoyance."[38] This covered ravine and the associated "caverns" formed a stoutly fortified and defended advance position, as noted on some of the maps.

Numerous reports also noted that during the battle and in retreat toward the river, Red Sticks sought refuge in natural overhangs created by erosion along the riverbanks.[39] Logs, brush, and other debris provided cover in these "caves" or eroded banks. None of these natural formations are noted on the maps. Some ensconced in these overhangs were able to escape during the night, but others met their untimely end when Jackson's men combed the battleground on the 28th.[40] Perhaps the most detailed account of the fighting there comes from John Coffee, who reported that after the Americans overran the barricade, "the few [Red Sticks] who survived" took refuge "under the banks of the river." Coffee's men "continued to find and kill untill it became too dark to see," allowing those few who were able to escape a chance to flee during the night.[41]

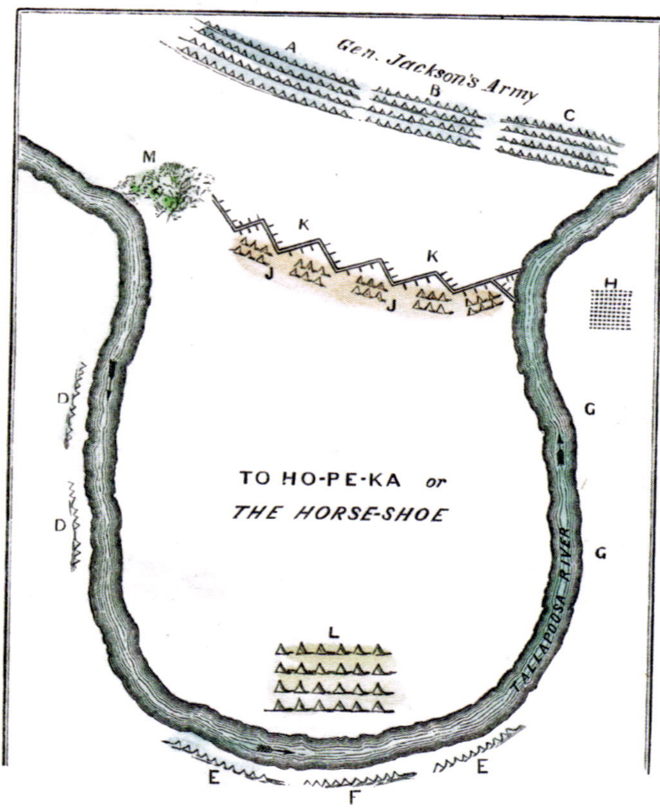

FIGURE 25. Engraved map produced in Charles E. Lester's *The Life of Sam Houston*. The map omits the island, and directional arrows indicate river flow is reversed. The map is significant for identification of the "Covered Ravine." Courtesy of the author.

Early park historians and archaeologists confused the "covered ravine" constructed at the declivity on the west end of the barricade with the naturally formed sheltering caves mentioned in Coffee's report and those featured in a dubious testimony reported by the nineteenth-century historian H. S. Halbert concerning Red Sticks killed the day after the battle by collapsing an overhang along the edge of the river. Glenn Hinsdale, the park's first historian, attempted to locate what he referred to as these "artificial caves." He turned to

> "an elderly resident who farmed the Horseshoe Bend prior to the turn of the century" for information about a possible location. This individual "took Mr. Hinsdale to two features in the east bank of the Horseshoe Bend peninsula which he believes are the remains of the caves. These extend from the flood plain to a point ⅔ of the way up the steep 60-foot bank. They have a narrow opening at the lowest point, on the flood plain, and open to a maximum width of about twenty feet near the top. At present they are about 15 feet below present ground level near the top, showing some evidence of soil deposition in the depression.[42]

Examination by various NPS personnel resulted in agreement that the "features described were not the result of ground erosion" and hinted at Red Stick construction. Hinsdale hoped that archaeological research would result in "recovery of the remains of actual participants in the battle, together with their weapons and personal gear."[43] The mix-up of a fortified declivity on the west side of the barricade with features on a cliff bank on the east side of the battlefield ultimately resulted in an examination by archaeologist Roy Dickens, who reported the features "did not appear to warrant archeological attention" and he declined to proceed.[44]

As the final resting place for the Muscogee Creek dead, the battlefield is now considered a war memorial. Moreover, further archaeological investigation is also limited due to restrictions placed on ground-disturbing activities at sites that have been previously surveyed due to the cost of both the work and preservation of any artifacts discovered. Thus, future research about the Red Stick fortification's precise location, shape, and construction will of necessity need to rely more heavily on extant cartographic and documentary records and improvements in geophysical search methods. Evidence points to not simply a massive wall but a series of "fortified works" that included an artfully constructed fortification of horizontal logs fitted with portholes, brushworks with forward entrenchments, as well as secondary fallback positions behind the main structure. After the initial attack on the wall at 12:30 p.m., Jackson's men fought until sunset as they made their way through the "high ground" of the peninsula toward the river, ferreting out pockets of resistance by Red Sticks entrapped in constructed thickets, covered ditches, and by battle's end, cliff embankments later perceived as "caves," where, infamously, sixteen wounded combatants were killed the day after the battle.[45]

South boundary of Tennessee.
TENNESSEE R.
Huntsville
Muscle shoals
Elk R.
Miltons
Colbert's ferry
Buzzard's roost C.
Coldwater C.
Sweetwater C.
Cypress C.
Shoal C.
Town C.
Poplar C.
Purple C.
Huricane C.
Little R.
Long leaf C.
Flint R.
Limestone Cr.
Indian C.
Walnut C.
Cane C.
Deposit
Sweetwater Cr.
Crowtown
Black W.
M'Lamores
Willstown
Lookout mountains
COOSEE R.
Hightower
Ft. Armstrong
Rocky R.
Turkey's town
Wills Cr.
Shoal River
Burnt by Gen. Coffee
Littafutchee
Canoe Cr.
Partridge Cr.
Tallishatchee Cr.
Tallushatchee
Ft. Strother
Ft. Chimabee
Villages burnt by Maj. Conn
An Indian camp routed
Ft. Talladeegee
Coosee
Eufaula C.
Eufaula old T.
TALLAPOOSEE R.
Hatcheenula
Talcauga
Lutcheepoga
Chattahochee
TOMBIGBY RIVER
red bank
BLACK WARRIOR RIVER
Pattagohatchee Tuskaloosa Sipsoeakquema
Ft. Williams
Abacoochee
Natchez
Emuckfau
New york
Tohopeca
Old Horse path
Oaktuskee
Oakfuscoochee
Tallahasse
Tuckaubatchee Tallahasse
Upper Pensotau
Lower Pensotau
Oaknoxaby Cr.
Boxmakers C.
Old Fort Confederation
Bluff
Sockomatchee
black bluff
Oakchia Cr.
Chickasaw Bogue
CAWHABA RI
Ft. Jackson
Hickory Ground
Attauga

CHAPTER 3

Battle Maps as a Key to Understanding the Creek Response to the American Invasion

Although the maps have not been particularly helpful in determining the exact location or design of the Red Stick barricade, they are exceedingly powerful testament to the successful battle tactic employed by Andrew Jackson: surround and exterminate. General Ferdinand Claiborne attempted the same at the earlier Creek War battle of Eccanachaca (Holy Ground), but the terrain there prevented the American army from encircling that town. The defenses at Holy Ground, though not as impressive as those at Tohopeka, were strong enough to allow the defenders to protect their civilians until they could escape by river. At Horseshoe Bend, Jackson's execution was nearly flawless and the terrain was more favorable for the encirclement. At day's end, Jackson's men understood the importance of what they had achieved. Their maps memorialized the detailed plan of battle, executed more or less precisely, that won the day. The tactics are vividly displayed on the maps.

J. Brian Harley, the eminent historian of cartography, famously noted that maps, far from being representations of geographic reality, are "social construction[s] of the world expressed through the medium of cartography." Cartographers, by their selective representation and manner of presentation, construct powerful narratives that are inherently biased and scripted to represent the priorities of the artist. As Harley noted, maps "are a construction of reality, images laden with intentions and consequences."[1] As Jerry Brotton phrased it, "maps offer a proposal about the world, rather than just a reflection of it, and every proposal emerges from a particular culture's prevailing assumptions and preoccupations."[2] Maps are statements by their creators and reflect their priorities. This understanding of the purpose and power of cartography helps explain why the mapmakers focused on the outcome achieved by the victors rather than any interest in a precise description of the Indian "works." The fortification, once breached, became metaphorical, making an accurate representation unnecessary. On the maps of the victors, Tohopeka is portrayed not as an ingeniously and ably defended stronghold of enemy Red Sticks but as a symbol of American military success. The maps, in fact, are souvenirs and aide-mémoire for the victors themselves and those for whom they described their actions.

The maps speak to territorial appropriation at every level because the one thing generally lacking on the maps of the most important battle of the Creek War are the Red Sticks themselves. Only one map, drawn by an unnamed Tennessean, actually labels the enemy. And that label is telling: "Red sticks Running."[3] On the other maps, the enemy is largely absent, unlabeled. Their absence calls to mind Jackson's stated objective of "exterminating" the Creeks. On the ground, literally and figuratively, he succeeded. On the Jackson map, the army's Cherokee members are depicted, but the contingent of National Council Creeks fighting under the command of Major William McIntosh is not shown. There is an "Indian village," the Emuckfau battle site, and the location of the previously burned Creek town of "New Youcan."

FIGURE 26. Interpretative image showing the sharpshooters on Bean's Island. Courtesy of Horseshoe Bend National Military Park, National Park Service.

But Jackson's map includes no dotted lines or hash marks to indicate that the breastworks came fully equipped with human architects and defenders.[4] One might argue that the victors simply did not know the disposition of the enemy behind the barricade. It would be a hollow argument, for the Americans came to know the battleground exceedingly well, having fought past and later walked the field examining the enemy's secondary fallback positions. A precise rendering of the enemy and their fortifications is absent by choice. The maps confirm the opinion of Colonel William Carroll, who wrote to an unnamed friend, "I think it is the most complete victory that has been obtained over the Indians in America."[5] Andrew Jackson himself declared the victory was "complete and decisive."[6] Not only did Jackson's forces destroy the Red Stick army, but the victors excluded them from their maps and the American victory left a lasting imprint on the Creek landscape. The elevation from which Jackson's cannon fired is now known as Gun Hill.[7] The small island, once an Indian field, is now known as Bean's Island for the man commanding the sharpshooters stationed there.[8] *Tohopeka*, a Muskogee term that means fence or signifies a fort, is now relegated to the name of the "village" in the toe of the bend rather than as a term for the defensive works. All traces of Red Stick military activity have been erased from the landscape.

Two of the maps provide unlabeled recognition to those who fought the American force. Colonel Carroll's map uses dots to represent personnel, both American and Red Stick. On the Red Stick side of the breastwork, the enemy is represented by two neat rows of dots, with other dots sparsely inhabiting the high ground and the village. The dots are not labeled, although every other contingent on the map is clearly labeled. It is the only map to mention the presence of McIntosh's Creek regiment ("Friendly Creeks") and notes the location they crossed the Tallapoosa into the refugee village. On the map drawn by Lieutenant J. L. Holmes for Leonard Tarrant, an orderly series of red hash marks along the barricade and the top part of the peninsula hint at either secondary brushwork fortifications or enemy personnel while American features as well as the "Breast Work" and the river are drawn in black.

On the Tarrant map, like that of the unidentified Tennessean, red ink was employed to depict the enemy. It is tempting to view this as a symbolic depiction of the bloodshed. For as Alexander McCulloch, an aide to John Coffee, wrote home to his wife, "The Tallapoosa might be truly called a River of blood for the water was so stained that at 10 Oclock at night it was very perceptibly bloody so much that it could not be used." McCulloch, in his letter to his "D[ea]r Fransey," also enclosed "a plan of the bend of the River together with the fortifications and situations of both Infantry & cavalry." His battlefield drawing has not been located or positively identified.[9]

The most important question about the battle is one the maps do not address: Why did the Creeks choose to fortify that place? Was there spiritual significance to the site as some have posited? Perhaps. But the construction of the massive barricade testifies to the fact that they did not intend to depend solely on ritual and prophets to stop armies, bullets, and cannonballs. Quite the contrary, Red Stick military engineers expended considerable effort on the design and construction of the fortification using traditional techniques, and they did so over a short time. The enclosure's purpose was never addressed by Americans other than obliquely through their notions of the "town" or "houses" or "village" behind the "fort." But it is obvious that the great wall was designed to protect noncombatants assembled in a hastily constructed refugee village. On the various maps, the village is labeled variously as "New Yauca" or "Horse Shoe Town" (Carroll map), "Indian Village" (Jackson map), "Town" (McEwen and "Tahopta" maps), and "Tehoopcau" (Tarrant and Taylor maps). The remaining maps provide no captions, although most provide symbols for the habitations there. The representations of the structures vary in number and kind but do suggest log cabin construction of the sort beginning to become more common among the Creeks. The Stevens map is the only one to number the structures: "300 Houses."[10]

George Stiggins, a Natchez Creek Indian whose manuscript history of the Creek people is the sole account written from the Creek perspective, explained the reason that the Red Sticks abandoned their towns. In the late fall of 1813, at the onset of the American invasion, Jackson's forces destroyed a cluster of small towns in the northern part of the Creek territory. It was then, according to Stiggins, that the Creeks began to "think of manner and means by which they might evade a total annihilation of their nation." Scattered among dispersed and unfortified towns, they were defenseless and liable to be destroyed "piecemeal." After debate in councils, Red Stick leaders decided that "certain named towns should be selected and embraced . . . at particular places of natural strength and by such means those different stations or encampments would each separately be strong enough to contend with and repel any invading army that might attack them."[11]

Stiggins's brother-in-law, William Weatherford, was one of the great military leaders of the Red Stick movement. He and the Alabama Red Stick combatants chose to fortify Eccanachaca (Holy Ground). Far from relying solely on the "magic" so often cited by historians for defense, the Red Stick forces there held off the approaching American forces behind fortified positions while civilians were evacuated. At Holy Ground, ostensibly an American victory, there are no battlefield maps. What is most remembered (and celebrated) regarding that battle is Red Stick leader William Weatherford's escape by riding his horse off a steep bluff into the Alabama River. Americans would later glorify Weatherford's heroic horsemanship while at the same time boasting they had breached the "magic" perimeter established by the prophets. In reality, the Red Sticks, with their thoughtfully chosen defensive position, defensive brushworks, firepower, and resolve, managed to achieve their goal of preserving life as they held off the American advance, thereby allowing civilians to escape. The entire aim of the fortified refugee villages was not merely religious introspection but preservation of the civilian population.[12]

Tohopeka was clearly a defensive position meant to protect the village in the toe of the bend. Prior to the battle at Emuckfau Creek on January 22, one of Jackson's Creek spies reported that Red Sticks at a nearby encampment were evacuating women and children.[13] Given the relative number of women reported captured to men killed on the ground, it would appear that many were successfully evacuated prior to the battle, although the rapid encirclement by horsemen prevented the complete

FIGURE 27. Interpretative oil painting by Sidney King (1964) depicting the Tohopeka village. Courtesy of Horseshoe Bend National Military Park, National Park Service.

evacuation of noncombatants. The great Red Stick war leader Menawa, who managed to escape the battlefield during the night after having been left for dead, floated downstream under cover of darkness and was found by women who were waiting for evacuees from the battlefield.[14] Reports vary on the number of noncombatants captured, and Americans recorded very little about them in their reports and letters. Jackson wrote to his wife that "about" 350 women had been captured.[15] Other reports listed a higher number, but an accurate count proved impossible due to the actions of the allied Cherokees, who captured many of the Creek women and children and enslaved them. McIntosh's allied Creeks took possession of some women in a bid to protect them and demanded the return of captives, but no record remains of the number involved.[16]

Unlike many of the manuscript maps, the engraved map published in Sam Houston's memoir noted the location of the Creek defenders as well as the American army's Cherokee and Creek regiments (labeled "Friendly Indians"). The map places "Women and children" at the site of the previously destroyed village of Nuyaka. No reports place the noncombatants there at the start of the battle, but this may well have been the location where the prisoners—as well as Jackson's Cherokee and Creek soldiers—camped after the battle. The cabins in the toe of the bend were set on fire, and when Coffee's Cherokee and Creek soldiers rejoined the main army, they took their prisoners with them. Other maps as well as Coffee's report indicate that their withdrawal from the bend took them through Nuyaka, which had been burned in late 1813 by Georgia troops.

The Red Stick failure at Horseshoe Bend was not one of will, belief, planning, or suitable weaponry. Nor, as one historian has suggested, was it the fact that the Creek "war chiefs . . . had no conception of military objectives and were unable to give any direction to their war."[17] Rather, it was failure to anticipate the number of soldiers (three thousand) that Jackson would bring to bear allowing him to surround the peninsula and cut off escape by water. By March 1814, Jackson's forces had swelled enormously, and on the day of the battle, his forces outnumbered the Red Sticks three to one. The American maps proudly display the encirclement and deployment of firepower that cut off all means of escape. Except for the surviving noncombatants who were captured by the Cherokees, only a handful of Red Stick Creeks managed to leave the battlefield alive.

FIGURE 28. "For General Jackson's Campaign against the Creek Indians 1813 & 1814" was based on an original in the War Department. It is sometimes attributed to John Melish but was likely the work of Major Howell Tatum, who was Jackson's topographical engineer after Horseshoe Bend. Courtesy of the Alabama Department of Archives and History.

FIGURE 29. Portrait of Selocta by Henry Inman, oil on canvas, 30 5/16 × 25 1/4. Courtesy of the High Museum of Art, Atlanta; anonymous gift, 1984.173.

Selocta was the son of Chennabee, the mico of the Natchez town among the Upper Creeks and member of the National Council. When the Creek civil war erupted, Chennabee and his supporters "forted up" at Talladega and were surrounded by hostile Red Sticks. Selocta is generally credited with slipping through their encirclement and making it to Jackson's camp to solicit aid. Selocta and other Natchez warriors enrolled in Jackson's army in November 1813, and fought in all the major battles of the campaign. They also served as guides and "spies" running reconnaissance missions in advance of engagements. Selocta's brother, who also served in the American army, was killed just before Emuckfau. Thomas McKenney, director of the U.S. Bureau of Indian Affairs, described Selocta as "an intelligent and sagacious guide [to Jackson's army] during its marches, and a brave warrior and leader in battle." His name is rendered as Esholoctee on the Treaty of Fort Jackson, which ended the war, and is sometimes spelled Ishalakte. This portrait was copied by Henry Inman from the original produced from life by Charles Bird King, which was destroyed by fire in 1865 at the Smithsonian. That original was commissioned by Thomas McKenney of the 1825–1826 Creek treaty delegation to Washington, D.C. Quotation from Thomas L. McKenney and James Hall, *The History of the Indian Tribes of North America: With Biographical Sketches and Anecdotes of the Principal Chiefs . . .*, 2 vols. (Philadelphia, 1838), 2:194; painting info from Kathryn H. Braund, *The Indian Gallery of Henry Inman* (Jule Collins Smith Museum of Fine Art, Auburn University, 2008).

FIGURE 30. *Me-Na-Wa or The Great Warrior (Creek)* by Henry Inman, 1831–1834, oil on canvas, 30 × 25 inches. Collection of Ann and Tom Cousins, Atlanta, Georgia; photo courtesy of the High Museum of Art, Atlanta.

Menawa of Okfuskee, "The Great Warrior," remains the most celebrated Red Stick Creek who fought at Horseshoe Bend. He was wounded seven times during the battle, including a shot through the cheek. He managed to escape during the night by making his way to a canoe and floating downstream where Creek women evacuated earlier were waiting for survivors. After the war, he became one of the leading spokesmen for the Creek Nation. In one of history's great ironies, as a warrior and "law mender," Menawa was dispatched as head of the party sent by the Creek Nation to execute William McIntosh in 1825. McIntosh commanded the allied Creeks who lined the riverbanks with Coffee's contingent at Horseshoe Bend and at the time was highly regarded as one of the nation's bravest men. His support of a fraudulent treaty with the Americans (1825) that ceded all Creek land east of the Chattahoochee River to the state of Georgia resulted in his execution by the Creek Nation and, ultimately, the repudiation of that treaty by the United States. Menawa and Selocta were among the delegates sent to protest McIntosh's unauthorized treaty. This portrait is a copy of the original by Charles Bird King, who produced portraits of most of the delegation. King's originals were destroyed by fire in 1865.

CHAPTER 4

Memorializing Sacrifice

In a letter describing the battle, General William Bradford assured William Henry Harrison "that 557 Indians were found dead on the ground is a fact." But the exact number of Red Stick dead remains murky since many were shot and killed as they swam across the river attempting to escape the American encirclement. Estimates range from two hundred to three hundred dead in the water. Bradford testified to this as well: "That the river was red with blood from the number that was killed in it is equally true—I never witnessed such carnage."[1] The consensus, summed up loosely by John Coffee, was "not less 850, or 900," Red Sticks slain on March 27.[2]

Whereas the method whereby Jackson's officers obtained their precise count of enemy dead on land is unclear, the manner in which they recorded their own casualties is well known. Company officers searched for their men on the battlefield and made a careful record of the dead and wounded. As physicians cared for the American wounded, the army prepared its own dead for burial, which consisted of wrapping the corpses in blankets, weighing them down, and sinking them in the river.[3] Lieutenant James W. Sittler, who served as adjutant general, was tasked with compiling the casualty reports of various company officers. Sittler's detailed casualty list was published in the *Nashville Whig* on May 10, 1814. The report listed the dead and wounded by company.[4] Some of the severely wounded died after the battle. Per Sittler's final accounting, the American army had thirty-two dead and ninety-nine wounded. Allied Creek and Cherokee losses were also enumerated, and by April 5, Jackson reported that eighteen Cherokees had been killed with thirty-six wounded while five allied Creeks were killed and eleven were wounded, making his army's total dead fifty-five. He astutely reckoned his army's losses "a small number, when we consider the nature of the conflict and the loss of the enemy."[5]

The published casualty list provided news to concerned family and friends of the American soldiers and memorialized the names of the American dead, who had been denied the dignity of a proper burial. The list of names highlighted the much smaller percentage of American and allied casualties when compared with the massive (and anonymous) Red Stick losses, which were near total. The count provided hard, numerical proof of a "complete" victory over the enemy and, in no small way, was in itself a means of commemorating victory. The scale of the devastation to the Red Stick Creeks demonstrated the magnitude of their defeat and quantified the consequence of war against America.

Andrew Jackson had clearly stated his aim in attacking, and "determining to exterminate them," his men encircled the peninsula, outnumbering his enemy by a three-to-one ratio.[6] The American troops who breached the breastwork fought toward those attacking from the rear, pinning down the Red Stick defenders until, as Jackson's biographer succinctly noted, "the battle became, at length, a slow, laborious slaughter."[7] While the Americans celebrated their gallantry and memorialized their dead, there was only grudging acknowledgment of the heroism and determination on the part of the Red Sticks, who

FIGURE 31. A member of the Muscogee Creek Lighthorse Explorer program contemplates a luminary display placed by the National Park Service on the battlefield as part of the commemoration of the battle's bicentennial in 2014. The 557 Red Stick dead are represented to the right of the posts representing the barricade while 55 luminaries on the left represent the losses of the American forces. Photo courtesy of Kenneth Boone.

fought valiantly against impossible odds. Only one among them was named in Jackson's numerous reports: "their famous prophet Monahoee—shot in the mouth by grape shot; as if Heaven designed to chastise his impostures by an appropriate punishment."[8]

The sheer number of enemy dead had a profound impact on the American army. Being witnesses to such horrific bloodletting, the personal toll of witnessing such "carnage" seeps through in letters to family and friends. As does the pride in the totality of the American victory, which is plainly displayed on the maps of the battle. Isaac Stephens carefully recorded in the title of his map, "the Indians were totally destroyed by the unequalled bravery of the gallant Sons of Tennessee, commanded by General Jackson."[9]

The only death memorialized on any of the manuscript maps is that of Major Lemuel Purnell Montgomery, whose loss is noted on the Jackson map with a small circle near the Red Stick barricade and the words "That angle at which Mongomery fell."[10] The circle indicates the leading thrust of the Thirty-Ninth Regiment but, by the nature of the label, is more properly meant as a memorial to the fallen hero rather than an indication of the Thirty-Ninth Regiment's position.

In his letter to Tennessee governor Willie Blount, Jackson singled out the three officers of the Thirty-Ninth "who fell in the charge which was made on the works": Major Montgomery, First Lieutenant Robert M. Somerville, and Second Lieutenant Michael Moulton. Jackson assured Blount that "no men ever acted more gallantly, or fell more gloriously."[11] The deaths of all three would be remembered by the new state of Alabama: Moulton and Somerville became the names of new towns, and Montgomery was honored with the name of a new county carved from the postwar Creek land cession.[12]

FIGURE 32. Details from the Andrew Jackson map. Courtesy of the Tennessee State Archives.

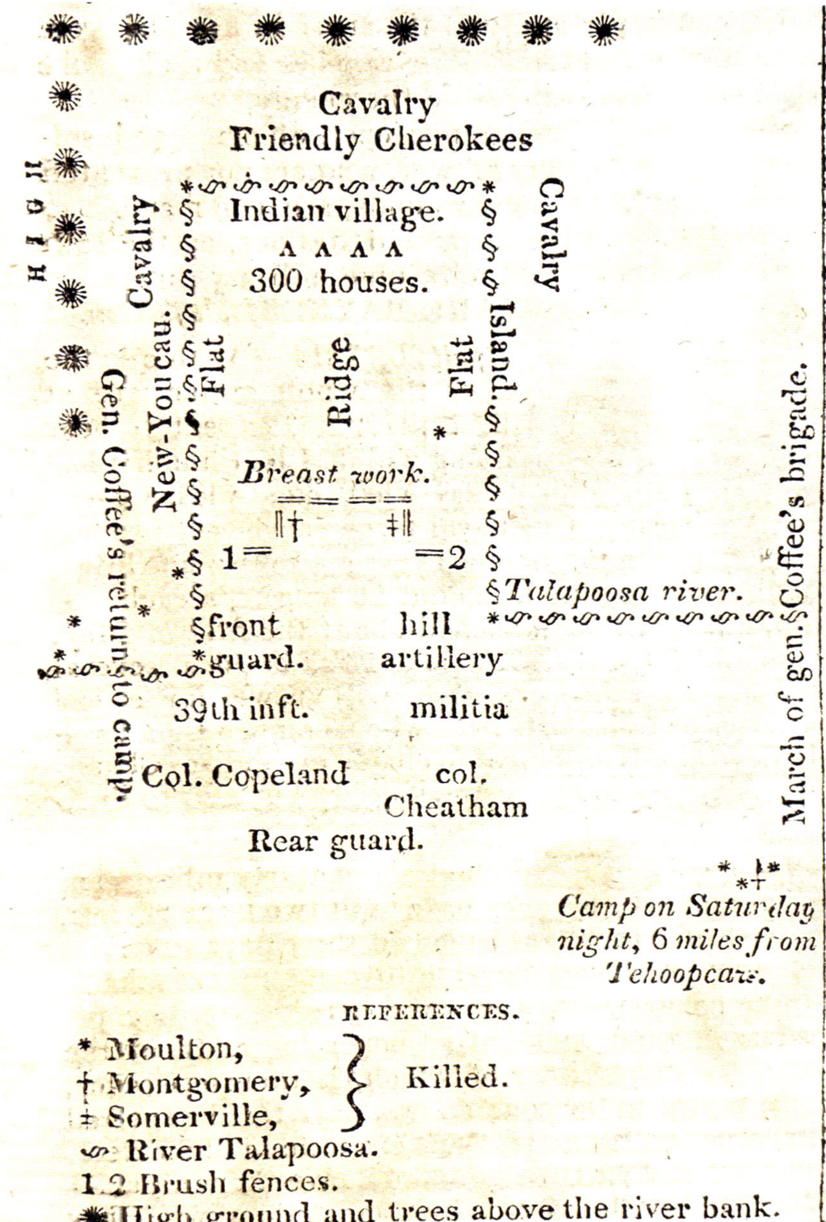

FIGURE 33. *A Draft of the Scene of the Action, Taken by an Officer on the Spot*, developed from a hand-drawn map and published in *Niles Weekly Register* on May 7, 1814, specifically noted the locations at which the three officers of the Thirty-Ninth Regiment were killed.

As the highest ranking officer to die, Montgomery's loss was singled out. Major John Reid, whose letter to an unnamed friend was published in a Nashville newspaper just over two weeks after the battle, gave no further details about Montgomery's death, other than noting he "fell in charging the works. He acted with the greatest gallantry."[13] The most explicit testimony of Montgomery's death came from the pen of John Coffee, who reported to his father-in-law that "Lemuel Montgomery was killed in the charge against the breast works, by a ball through his head, after he reached the wall, he fired his pistol through a port hole, and killed an Indian and in an instant afterwards was shot through the same hole, and fell dead—never spoke."[14] Major Reid, Jackson's aide-de-camp, related the same to his wife: "shot dead at the wall—having just killed an Indian through a port hole with his pistol."[15] John Donelson Jr. sent word to his father that Montgomery "fell gallantly chargeing at the head of his men."[16] Alexander McCulloch also noted the major's demise, telling his wife that Montgomery "no[bly died] at the enemy's fortifications waving his hat an [huzzai]ng when he received a ball in the head which instantly killed him."[17]

Montgomery's heroism and blood sacrifice came to stand for the conduct and loss of all those who had died and for the fact that, as Jackson noted, "every officer and man did his duty." He was emphatic that "never was more heroism or roman courage displayed."[18] Jackson's commemoration of Montgomery's death, as well as the fact that he was the only American honored with a military interment on the battlefield, linked the self-sacrifice of an officer to earlier patriots, whose service and deaths had elevated them to heroes during the American Revolution. The transformation of Montgomery's death from battlefield statistic to a symbol of self-sacrifice as well as the extra tokens of respect given his remains replicate those afforded to Colonel Joseph Hamilton Daveiss, who was killed at the Battle of Tippecanoe. Daveiss was buried "'at a distance'" from the other fallen American soldiers of that battle. And following his ceremonial interment, his comrades obscured his grave by first burning brush and then concealing the site with leaves. The mass grave of the other American dead at Tippecanoe was later desecrated by Indians and the bodies scalped. Jackson prevented a replication of that insult by sinking the bodies of other dead Americans in the Tallapoosa River. Montgomery's body, like that of Daveiss, was disinterred and later moved to another burial site.[19]

Lemuel Montgomery's sacrifice was almost immediately linked to that of a far more renowned hero: Richard Montgomery. Jackson would later pay regards to General Richard Montgomery's aged widow and note his esteem for her dead husband, the "revered" patriot.[20] In Alabama, the names of both men are memorialized as a county (Major Montgomery) and a city (General Montgomery) and Major Montgomery is claimed as one of Alabama's earliest and most noble heroes.[21] Albert J. Pickett, Alabama's most noted early historian, declared Montgomery to have been "altogether, the finest looking man in the army." In his two-volume history of the state published in 1851, Pickett embellished Montgomery's actions and literally elevated his demise, asserting that the major "was the first man that mounted the breast-work, and, while waving his sword and animating his men, a large ball, shot from the rifle of a Red Stick, entered his head, and instantly killed him. When the battle was ended, Jackson stood over his body, and wept. He exclaimed, 'I have lost the flower of my army!'"[22] This version of the major's death is the one that has, as historian Tom Kanon noted, "remained fixed in the public's memory of the battle."[23]

The major's death at the Red Stick breastwork elevated his standing over his commander, Colonel John Williams, whom Jackson described as "skillful and intrepid."[24] A letter submitted by "a distinguished officer" to the Nashville *Clarion* specifically called out the Thirty-Ninth Regiment's performance, noting that "it was an admirable charge. Col. Williams is a sterling officer" as well as noting the death of Montgomery.[25] Indeed, Williams was likely the first to reach the Creek barricade.[26]

The image, however flawed, of a handsome, gallant, and well-connected officer, sword aloft, bravely leading the charge against the Red Stick barricade quickly became an iconic symbol of "the unequalled bravery of the gallant Sons of Tennessee" as well as the new state of Alabama.[27] So determined were they to commemorate Montgomery's sacrifice that the state of Alabama organized a militia detail to locate the major's battlefield resting place shortly after the removal of the Creeks from the area following another brief war against them in 1836.[28] In the spring of 1839, a brigade of Alabama militia volunteers converged on the site and located the major's remains. They were assisted by a veteran of the battle and an enslaved man, then living nearby, who had accompanied the army and "acted as drummer at the funeral." After some effort, the Alabamians discovered the remains and, by "the indication of a bullet hole through the skull, proved them, beyond question, to be the remains of Montgomery." The bones were collected and transported to newly established Dudleyville, the closest town to the battle site, for reburial with proper military honors on the town's main street.[29] An effort by the Alabama legislature to approve $500 for the erection of a monument to Major Montgomery failed.[30] Over time, Dudleyville sank into obscurity, and the grave was all but lost until the late nineteenth century, when heavy rains exposed bones, believed by the landowner to be those of Montgomery. These remains were collected and reburied. In 1933, the Tohopeka Chapter of the Daughters of the American Revolution (DAR) marked the site with a stone monument, which by that time was in a cow pasture rather than a thriving settlement.[31] Following the establishment of the battle site as a national military park, efforts were again made to locate Montgomery's remains due to strong local enthusiasm to commemorate the major's heroic sacrifice for his country. Newspaper accounts singled out his "gallantry" and status as a "distinguished lawyer" and army officer. Park personnel conducted research on the removal of the major's remains and reburial, and ultimately, a "Major Montgomery Commemorative Committee" was established. In 1972, the major was again disinterred by a team of NPS archaeologists, and the few remaining bone fragments and teeth located were placed into a satin-lined casket. These were reburied in a public ceremony at the park on June 12. The original DAR marker was also relocated to mark his new resting place.[32] In 1987, Montgomery County, Alabama, named for the fallen hero, erected a statue at the county's courthouse depicting Montgomery "drawing his sword moments before his death."[33]

The veneration of the dead major was not limited to Alabama. John Frost's 1846 biography of Andrew Jackson featured two engravings to depict the battle at Horseshoe Bend. The first showed the American army planting the cannon prior to bombardment and the second showed a stricken Montgomery, standing at the Red Stick barricade, dropping his sword.[34] Montgomery's grave continues to be the focus of patriotic remembrance and veneration. He is widely identified as not only the "first" death at the battle but also erroneously credited as the man who led the charge, and his story continues to play a prominent role in the interpretation of the battle at the national park. His monument and grave site were the focus of commemorative activities honoring the American dead during the bicentennial of the battle in 2014.[35]

The battle at Horseshoe Bend was a signal American victory and a crushing blow to the Creek people. It was also a complete and total victory that transformed the mental tableau of the American people. The Red Stick Creeks, in defeat, disappeared from both mind and map to be replaced by a celebration of heroic sacrifice, military prowess, and American dominance. The maps and monuments of the victors are testimony to that point of view. As the victors walked the field the day after the battle, they collected souvenirs from the bodies of the dead. Jackson procured "a warriors bow & quiver" for his adopted son Andrew.[36] One account claimed the Americans flayed the skin of fallen Creeks to make wallets and belts—a most savage means of demonstrating mastery over the defeated.[37] Later accounts would report pipes, "rings," and other objects taken from the dead, but none have been located to date. Not a single red stick—the emblematic enemy weapon—graces the collection of an American museum. It comes as no surprise that two weapons that did see action on March 27, 1814, and still survive belonged to Major Lemuel Montgomery. The Tennessee State Museum displays Montgomery's sword, while his American-made .38-caliber pistol is housed at the Smithsonian's National Museum of American History.[38]

The gun was featured for a time in a web exhibit titled "The Price of Freedom."[39] One might more properly have called that particular part of the exhibit "The Price of Winning Indian Territory." The exhibit inaccurately portrayed the Creek War as one "against the United States," when, in fact, it was a war of

FIGURE 34. Montgomery dropping his sword at the barricade after his fatal wound. From John Frost, *A Pictorial Biography of Andrew Jackson* (New York, 1860). Montgomery's sword is is part of the Tennessee Historical Society Collection at the Tennessee State Museum, Nashville.

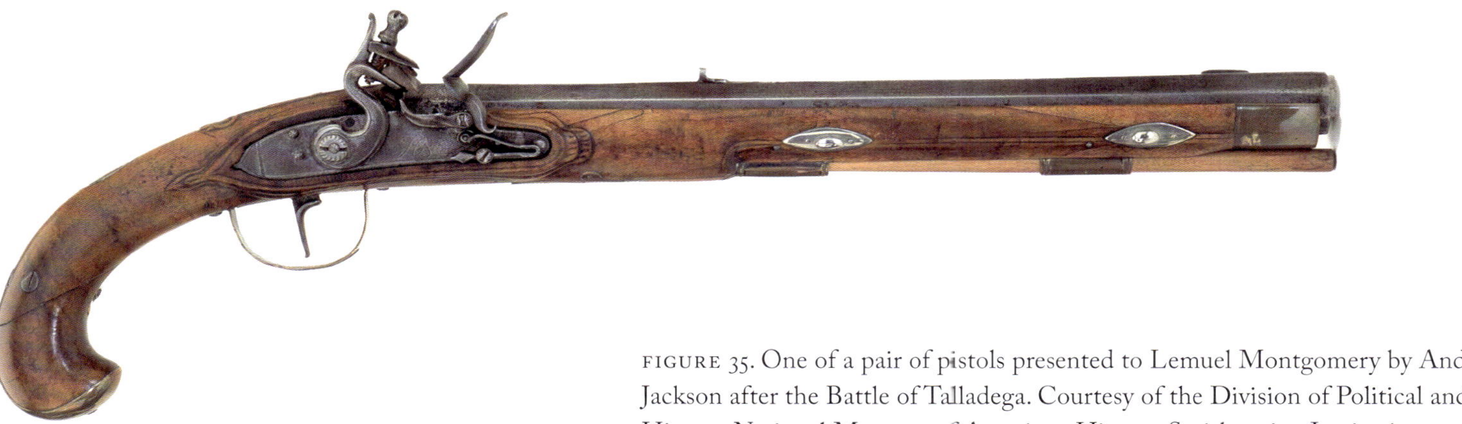

FIGURE 35. One of a pair of pistols presented to Lemuel Montgomery by Andrew Jackson after the Battle of Talladega. Courtesy of the Division of Political and Military History, National Museum of American History, Smithsonian Institution.

Americans against a faction of the Creek Nation. There is no mention of the fact that one of the outcomes of Montgomery's death and Jackson's victory was the acquisition of 21,086,793 acres of Creek territory—shifted to the American side of the boundary on postwar maps.[40]

American soldiers produced an amazing array of visual representations of the Battle of Horseshoe Bend as souvenirs, as a way to explain and commemorate their great victory, to celebrate heroism, and to venerate heroes. Their maps were more than artifacts of a successful military operation or primers for military intelligence, although a few were expressly made for that purpose. Many were clearly designed to be presentation items for those with an interest in the war and military affairs. The maps, at their most elementary level, are souvenirs for men of certain social standing and rank meant to memorialize gallantry, duty, service, and blood sacrifice. The maps, by their distribution to family, friends, and colleagues, represent the sense of pride that the officers felt in their achievement in arms as well as their roles in the victory. The continuing celebrations of "gallantry" and victory at "the Horse-Shoe" among officers and men in Tennessee that continued years after the event no doubt aided in the preservation of the maps produced by veterans of the battle.[41]

In our own day, archaeologists have used the battlefield maps in various attempts to determine the site of the Red Stick barricade and to discern its design. Historians have been slow to do more than employ the maps as illustrations. It is time we paid heed to the cartographic record. The amateur maps reveal the mindset of the victors and the manner in which the American army achieved total victory. More important, they are essential to explaining the Red Stick side of the story. American maps highlight the fact that Red Stick defensive strategy centered on the protection of their civilian population. For whatever other reasons the peninsula was chosen, the impressive fortification erected in defense of a refugee village provides silent testimony that protection from an attacking army was a paramount consideration. The maps with their wildly varying renderings of the impressive defensive works explain not only how the battle unfolded but also how Red Stick aims shaped the kind of battle it was, why it took place where it did, and why the defenders fought to the last man—to save their families.

Fr. T. XXIII. R. XXIII. E. Land District Southe
Notes of this line see vol 56 page 394
Notes of the Sectional lines of this Township See vol 56 page 396 to 4
Notes of this line see vol 56 page 393
Notes of this line see vol 56 page 378
642.84 6
641.40 5
641.60 4
640 3
637.52 2
637.12 1
641.80 7
639.60 8
626.50 9
640.88 10
641.56 11
640.36 12
641.72 18
639.46 17
16
449.75 15
14
13
282.16 19
498.70 20
629.25 21
442.30 22
640.44 23
477.10 24
641.04 30
641.16 29
641.60 28
642.20 27
640.20 26
25
641.40 31
642.12 32
642.40 33
640.64 34
638.84 35
637.40 36
Emucfau creek
Tallapoosa River
Long Jim
Ac. 253.85
Molly
Ac. 208.00
Fi-e-char
Kan-no-ho-re
Ac. 156.50
Sec Comm.rs
April 24 184
Total area 22045.82 acres

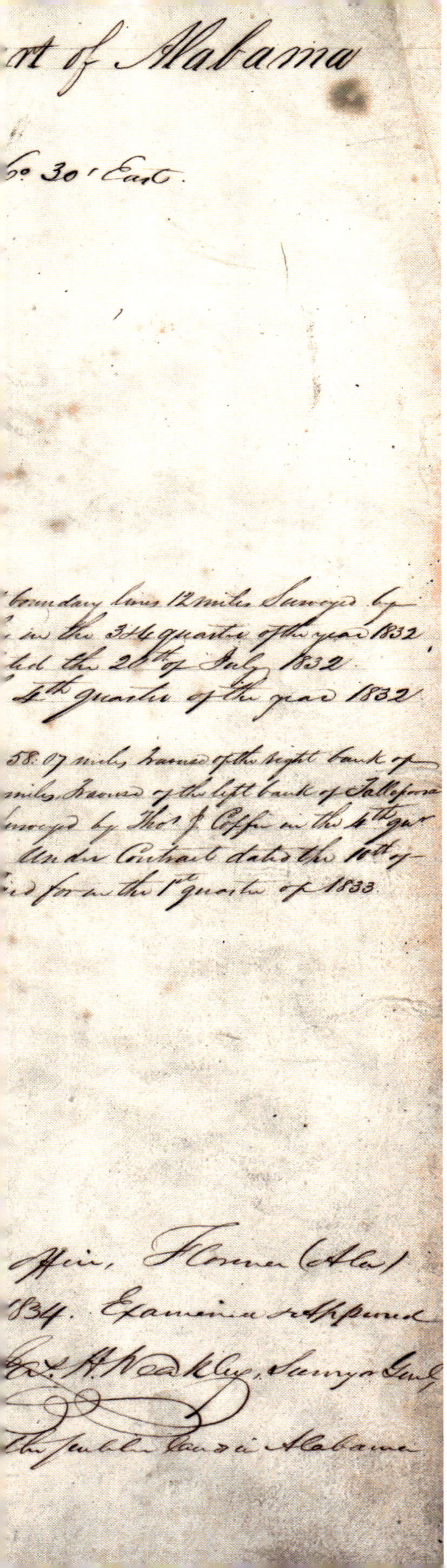

FIGURE 36. Detail of survey for Township 23, Range 23 in Tallapoosa County, Alabama, completed 1834, after the transfer of Creek land to American control under the Treaty of Washington, 1832. Courtesy of the Alabama Department of Archives and History.

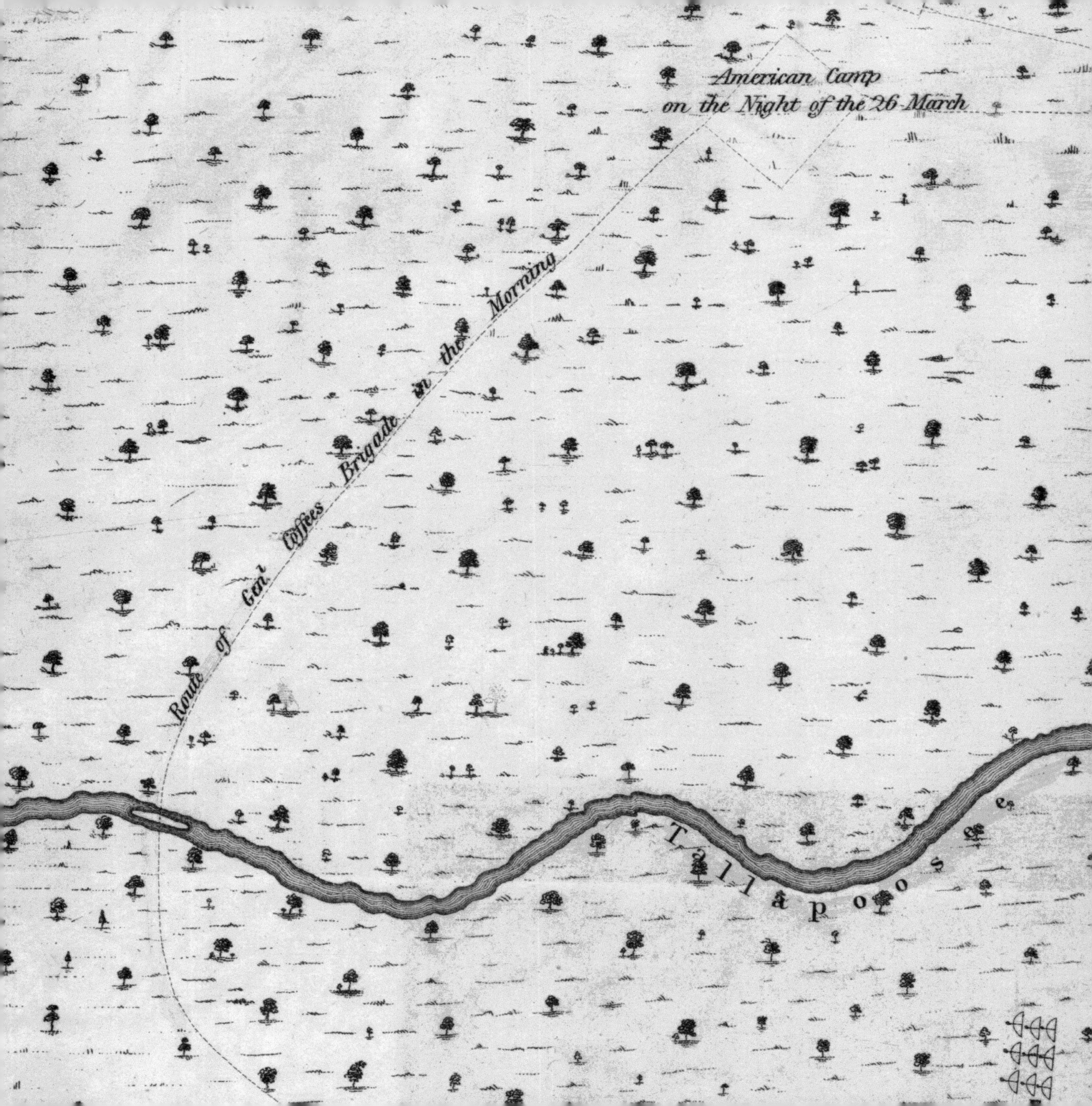

American Camp
on the Night of the 26 March
Route of Genl Coffees Brigade in the Morning
Tallapoosee

CHAPTER 5

Participant Accounts of the Battle of Horseshoe Bend

Immediately after leaving the battlefield, the American army returned to Fort Williams. From there, the officer corps dispatched official reports and letters to Nashville, directed to the War Department, the governor of Tennessee and other officials, as well as to wives, friends, and relatives. The letters were carried from the field by express riders and members of the army returning to Tennessee. Major William McIntosh, who commanded the allied regiment of Creek Indians, relayed most of the letters carried from the battlefield on March 28.[1] Many of the letters—both official and private—were also printed widely in newspapers.

The letters reveal the many personal relationships and family connections of the officers and their families. They also reveal the narrative constructed by the officer corps, with many of the letters using the same language to describe events. Employing the language of the day, they offer brutal and straightforward accounts of the battle, concentrating on their victory and losses, particularly among the officers. Although the letters are often repetitious, they are also valuable for their emphasis as well as specifics not found in other accounts. The letters in the first group represent the majority of the known primary accounts of the battle by Andrew Jackson and his officers, whose reports were preserved in official or family records. The letters in each group are arranged in chronological order, then alphabetically by sender. The second group of documents contains personal accounts by wounded veterans—two Americans and one Cherokee—who described their participation in the battle in order to obtain pensions. A supporting letter for another American veteran written by Jackson is also included. Such pension applications provide an insight into the individual experiences of those engaged in the conflict rather than the general descriptions of the army's success and highlight the vast gulf between officer and enlisted men. They detail the fighting along the barricade, noting enemy weapons and tactics. Surviving Red Sticks did not produce written accounts of their experience, but their oral testimony is captured in several documents and is included here for completeness as section III.

Letters and Reports from the Officer Corps

I. Andrew Jackson to Major General Thomas Pinckney

On the Battle ground on bend of the
Tallapoosa 28th March 1814[2]

Sir,

I feel peculiarly happy in being able to announce to you the fortunate eventuation of my expedition to the Tallapoosa. I reached the bend near Emuckfau (called by the whites the horse shoe) about ten OClk in the forenoon of yesterday, where I found the strength of the neighboring towns collected. Expecting our approach, they had gathered in from Oakfuskee, Oakchoya, New Youka Hillabees, the Fish-pond, & Eufaula towns,[3] to the number it is said of a thousand.

FIGURE 37. William McIntosh. Influential, wealthy, and a renowned warrior from the lower Creek town of Coweta, McIntosh led a regiment of nearly one hundred Creeks during the battle. They crossed the Tallapoosa, fighting their way through the village and into the high ground until nightfall. McIntosh attempted to take possession of captive Creek women and children to prevent their enslavement by the Cherokees and Americans with some success. Life-size portrait attributed to Nathan and Joseph Negus, 1821. Courtesy of the Alabama Department of Archives and History.

It is difficult to conceive a situation more eligible for defence than the one they had chosen, or one rendered more secure by the skill with which they had erected their breast work, it was from five to eight feet high, and extended across the point in such a direction, as that a force approaching it, would be exposed to a double fire while they lay in perfect security behind. A cannon planted at one extremity could have raked it to no advantage.

Determining to exterminate them, I detached Genl. [John] Coffee & nearly the whole of the Indian force, early on the morning of yesterday to cross the river about two miles below their encampment, & to surround the bend in such a manner, as that none of them should escape by attempting to cross the river; With the infantry I proceeded slowly & in order along the point of land which led to the front of their breast work. Having planted my cannon (one six & one three pounder[)] on an eminence at the distance of one hundred & fifty or to two hundred yds from it, I opened a very brisk fire, playin upon the enemy with the musquetry & rifles whenever they shewed themselves beyond it. This was kept up with short interruptions for about two hours, when a part of the Indian force & Capn. [William Russell] Russels & Lt [Jesse] Beans companies of Spies, who had accompanied Genl. Coffee crossed over in canoes to the extremity of the bend & set fire to a few of the buildings which were there situated, they then advanced with great gallantry towards the breast work & commenced a spirited fire upon the enemy behind it. Finding that this force, notwithstanding the bravery they displayed was wholly insufficient to dislodge them, and that Genl. Coffee had entirely secured the opposite bank of the river, I now determined to take their works by storm. The men by whom this was to be effected, had been waiting with impatience to receive the order, & hailed it with acclamation. The spirit which animated them was a sure augury of the success which was to follow, the history of warfare furnishes few instance of a more brilliant attack. The Regulars led on by their skillful & intrepid commander Col [John] Williams & by the gallant Major [Lemuel] Montgomery soon gained possession of the works in the midst of a most tremendous fire from behind them. The militia of the venerable Genl Dohertys brigade accompanied them in the charge, with a vivacity & firmness which would have done honor to Regulars. The enemy were compleatly routed. Five hundred & fifty seven were left dead upon the peninsula, & a great number were killed by the horsemen; It is believed not more than 20 have escaped; The fighting continued with some severity for five hours, but we continued to destroy many of them until we were prevented by the night; This morning we killed sixteen who had lain concealed. We took about two hundred & fifty prisoners all women & children except two or three.

Our loss is 106 wounded & twenty six killed Major [William] McIntosh (the Coweta)[4] who joined my army with a part of his tribe greatly distinguished himself. When I get an hours leisure I will send you a more detailed account. According to my original purpose I commence my return march to Fort Williams today, & shall if I find sufficient supplies there hasten to the hicory ground.[5] The power of the creeks is I think forever broken.

I send you a hasty sketch taken by the eye of the situation in which the enemy were encamped, & of the manner in which I approached them.

I have the honor to be, with great respect
your Obt Servt
Andrew Jackson
Major Genl.

Source: Records of the Office of the Secretary of War, Record Group 107, Letters Received by the Secretary of War, Main Series, 1801–1870, National Archives. This letter was published widely in contemporary newspapers and appears in *The Papers of Andrew Jackson*, vol. 3: *1814–1815*, 52–53.

II. "Extract of a letter from a distinguished officer, dated 6 miles from New Youchaw, March 29, 1814"

On the 27th we reached the fortified bend of Tallapoosee, and attacked the Indians in that place half after ten o'clock—their situation was a military one admirably calculated for defence, their fortification was so strong that it was found impracticable to reduce it with the cannon—it was therefore found necessary to take it by storm, the 39th regiment and part of the militia charged and took possession of the breast works, and after a severe contest of a few minutes the Indians were driven back. The Cherokees in the mean time had crossed the river below and came in their rear. The slaughter was great, the battle continued until sun down. at which time the savages were all put to death, except a few that concealed themselves under the bank of the river. During the night they made their escape by swimming the river. The number found dead of the enemy 557 with the addition of at least 200 shot in the river—our loss, friendly Indians, Cherokee's, in all about 40 killed and 90 wounded. Major [Lemuel] Montgomery, of the regulars, was killed in the charge—it was an admirable charge. Col. [John] Williams is a sterling officer.

KILLED.

Capt. [Nicholas] Gibbs, Capt. Gains, and Capt. Carr.

WOUNDED.

James Lewis, Wm. Dew, John Allen, Alex Lard, Jesse Wilkinson, Col. [Gideon] Morgan, Capt. Hermes, Lieut. [Benjamin] Reynolds, and Lieut. Wright.[6]

Source: Printed in the *Clarion and Tennessee State Gazette*, Nashville, Tennessee, Tuesday, April 12, 1814.

III. "Copy of a letter from Major Reed [John Reid][7] to his friend in this place, dated Camp March 29"

We have at last struck a decisive blow. We found the enemy on the 27th to the number of one thousand, encamped on the bend of the Tallapoosee. You cannot imagine a situation more eligible for defence or rendered more secure by art.

Their breast work of compactness and strength, and from five to six feet high, extended across the point, in such a direction as that an enemy approaching would be exposed to a double fire. After finding it impracticable to make a breach in it with our cannon, we determined upon taking possession of it by storm. The enemy lay in great numbers and perfect security behind, awaiting our approach. Never were men more anxious to be led to the charge than both our regulars & militia. The long roll was sounded, and they moved forward to the charge with an undauntedness which was altogether astonishing. The breast work was soon ours—and then commenced on our side the work of destruction—The enemy were wholly routed—557 warriors were left dead on the Peninsula, besides a great number who were killed in the river in endeavoring to make their escape, by the cavalry who had been previously posted on the opposite bank of the river.—It is believed that very few escaped. We took 3 or 400 prisoners, women and children.

Our loss was 25 killed and 106 wounded, many of them mortally. Poor Major [Lemuel] Montgomery, whose death I sincerely lament, fell in charging the works. He acted with the greatest gallantry.

Source: Printed in the *Clarion and Tennessee State Gazette*, Nashville, Tennessee, Tuesday, April 12, 1814.

IV. Maj. Gen. Andrew Jackson to His Excellency Willie Blount

Ft. Williams, 31st. March 1814

Sir,

I am just returned from the expedition which I advised you in my last I was about to make to the Tallapoosa; & hasten to acquaint you with the good fortune which attended it.

I took up the line of march from this place on the morning of the 24th. Inst, & having opened a passage of fifty two & a half miles, over the ridges which divide the waters of the two rivers, I reached the bend of the Tallapoosa, three miles beyond where I had the engagements of the 22d. January & at the southern extremity of New Youka, on the morning of the 27th. This bend resembles, in its curvature that of a horse-shoe, & is thence called by that name among the Whites. Nature furnishes few situations so eligible for defence; & barbarians have never rendered one more secure by art. Across the neck of land which leads into it from the North, they had erected a breast-work, of greatest compactness & strength—from five to eight feet high, & prepared with double rows of port-holes very artfully arranged. The figure of this wall, manifested no less skill in the projectors of it, than its construction: an army could not approach it without being exposed to a double & cross-fire from the enemy who lay in perfect security behind it. The area of this peninsular, thus bounded by the breastwork includes, I conjecture, eighty or a hundred acres.

In this bend the warriors from Oakfuskee, Oakchoya, New-Youka, Hillabees, the Fish-ponds—& Eufaula towns, apprised of our approach, had collected their strength. Their exact number cannot be ascertained; but it is said, by the prisoners we have taken, to have been a thousand. It is certain they were very numerous; & that relying with the utmost confidence upon their strength—their situation—& the assurances of their prophets, they calculated on repulsing us with great ease.

Early on the morning of the 27th—having encamped the preceding night at the distance of six miles from them—I detached Genl. [John] Coffee with the mounted men & nearly the whole of the Indian force, to pass the river at a ford about three miles below their encampment, & to surround the bend in such a manner that none of them should escape by attempting to cross the river. With the remainder of the forces I proceeded along the point of land which led to the front of their breastwork; & at half past ten Oclk A. M. I had planted my artillery on a small eminence, distant from its nearest point about eighty yards, & from its farthest, about two hundred & fifty; from whence I immediately opened a brisk fire upon its centre. With the musquetry & rifles I kept up a galling fire whenever the enemy shewed themselves behind their works, or ventured to approach them. This was continued, with occasional intermissions, for about two hours, when Capt [William] Russells company of Spies & a part of the Cherokee force, headed by their gallant Chieftain Col. Richard Brown, & conducted by the brave Col. [Gideon] Morgan, crossed over to the extremity of the peninsula in Canoes, & set fire to a few of their buildings which were there situated. They then advanced with great gallantry towards the breastwork, & commenced firing upon the enemy who lay behind it.

Finding that this force notwithstanding the determined bravery they displayed, was wholly insufficient to dislodge the enemy & that Genl. Coffee had secured the opposite banks of the river, I now determined upon taking possession of their works by storm.

Never were men better disposd for such an undertaking than those by whom it was to be effected. They had entreated to be lead to the charge with the most pressing importunity, & received the order which was now given, with the strongest demonstration of joy. The effect was such, as this temper of mind, foretold. The regular troops, led on by their intrepid & skillful commander Col [John] Williams, & by the gallant Major [Lemuel] Montgomery were presently in possession of the nearer side of the breast-work; & the militia accompanied them in the charge with a vivacity & firmness which could not have been exceeded & has seldom been equalled by troops of any description. A few companies of Genl. [George] Doherty's Brigade on the right, were led on with great gallantry by Col. [Samuel] Bunch—the advance guard, by the Adjutant Genl. Col [James W.] Sit[t]ler, & the left extremity of the line by Capt [John] Gordan of the Spies, & Capt [James] McMurry, of Genl. [Thomas] Johnston's Brigade of West Tennessee Militia.

Having maintained for a few minutes a very obstinate contest, muzzle to muzzle, through the port-holes, in which many of the enemy's balls were welded to the bayonets of our musquets, our troops succeeded in gaining possession of the opposite side of the works. The event could no longer be doubtful. The enemy altho many of them fought to the last with that kind of bravery desperations inspires, were at length entirely routed & cut to pieces. The whole margin of the river which surrounded the peninsular was strewed with the slain. Five hundred & fifty seven were found by officers of great respectability whom I had ordered to count them; besides a very great number who were thrown into the river by their surviving friends, & killed in attempting to pass by Genl. Coffee's men, stationed on the opposite banks. Capt [Eli] Hammonds who with his company of Spies occupied a favourable position opposite the upper extremity of the breastwork, did great execution; & so did Leuit [Jesse] Bean, who had been ordered by Genl. Coffee to take possession of a small Island fronting the lower extremity.

Both officers & men who had the best opportunities of judging, believe the loss of the enemy in killed, not to fall short of eight hundred, & if their number was as great as it is represented to have been, by the prisoners, & as it is believed to have been by Col Carrol & others who had a fair view of them as they advanced to the breastworks, their loss must even have been *more* considerable—as it is quite certain that not more than twenty can have escaped. Among the dead was found their famous prophet Monahoee—shot in the mouth by a grape shot; as if Heaven designed to chastise his impostures by an appropriate punishment. Two other prophets were also killed—leaving no others, as I learn, on the Tallapoosa.

I lament that two or three women & children were killed by accident.

I do not know the exact number of prisoners taken; but it must exceed three hundred—all women & children except three or four.

The battle may be said to have continued with severity for about five hours; but the firing & the slaughter continued until it was suspended by the darkness of the night. The next morning it was resumed, & sixteen of the enemy slain who had concealed themselves under the banks.

Our loss was twenty six white men, killed, & one hundred & seven wounded—Cherokees, eighteen killed, & thirty six wounded—friendly Creeks 5 killed and 11 wounded.

The loss of Col [John] Williams' regt of Regulars is seventeen killed & fifty five wounded; 3 of whom have since died. Among the former were Maj Montgomery, Leuit [Robert M.] Somerville, & Leuit [Michael] Moulton, who fell in the charge which was made on the works.[8] No men ever acted more gallantly, or fell more gloriously.

Of the Artillery company, commanded by Capt Parish, eleven were wounded; one of whom, Saml [Samuel] Gaines, has since died; Leutinants [John] Allen & [Henry] Ridley were both wounded. The whole company acted with its usual gallantry. Capt [William] Bradford, of the 17th U.S. Infantry, who acted as chief engineer, & superintended the firing of the cannon, has entitled himself, by his good conduct, to my warmest thanks.

To say all in a word the whole army who achieved this fortunate victory, have merited by their good conduct, the gratitude of their country. So far as I saw, or could learn there was not an officer or soldier who did not perform his duty with the utmost fidelity. The conduct of the militia on this occasion has gone far towards redeeming the character of that description of troops. They have been as orderly in their encampments & on the line of march, as they have been signally brave in the day of battle.

In a few days I shall take up the line of march for the Hickory Ground; & have every thing to hope from such troops.

Enclosed I send you Genl Coffee's Brigade report.

I have the honor to be with great respect Your Obt St

Andrew Jackson Major Genl

Source: The original letter, with an accompanying map, was presented to the Tennessee Historical Society by R. T. Quarles in 1884. The letter—with slight variations—has been published numerous times, first in the April 12, 1814, edition of the *Clarion and Tennessee State Gazette* and more recently in John Spencer Bassett, ed., *Correspondence of Andrew Jackson*, 2 vols. (Washington, D.C.: Carnegie Institution, 1926), 1:489–92. Scholars generally identify the handwriting as that of Major John Reid, while the document is signed by Jackson. The bound copy is available online at https://teva.contentdm.oclc.org/digital/collection/p15138coll33/id/252/rec/39.

V. "Extract of a letter from Col. Wm. Carroll, to his friend in Nashville, dated Fort Williams April 1st. 1814"

At half past ten o'clock in the morning of the 27th of March we attacked the strong fortified bend of the Tallapoosee river—Gen. Coffee with the mounted men and Cherokees, had been detached in the morning to cross above and below the fortification to prevent the escape of the enemy by swimming the river. They had made a strong breast work across the bend, taking every military advantage the ground would afford. We opened a cannonade on them with a six and three pounder, but had little impression on their works, having attracted the attention of most of the Indians at the breast work the Cherokees and [William] Russels spies crossed the river and commenced an attack on their rear, at this moment the 39th regiment and part of the militia charged and took possession of the breast works, in this charge Major [Lemuel] Montgomery, of the 39th regiment was killed. Our loss is killed 49, wounded 154, Cherokees, friendly Creeks and whites all included.

The enemy lost about 800, 558 were found on the ground and upwards of 200 shot in the river attempting to swim it. I think it is the most complete victory that has been obtained over the Indians in America.

I escaped unhurt through all the battle till about half an hour before night, I was then wounded slightly in the left side, I find a little inconvenience from it now; I hope to be able to go to the hickory ground to which place we set out in a few days. I hope to return in about two weeks. We have much business to do, I have been writing wounded and sore as I am all day.

Source: Printed in the *Clarion and Tennessee State Gazette*, Nashville, Tennessee, Tuesday, April 12, 1814.

VI. John Coffee to his father-in-law, Captain John Donelson, in Davidson County, Tennessee

Fort Williams 1st April 1814

Dear Sir,

On the 17th. of March we left fort Strother, and marched to this post which is on the Coosey River, Sixty miles by land below fort Strother and about 15 degrees west of south from that place—On the 24th. we left this place and marched about 8 or ten degrees to the south of East, fifty two miles to the bend of the Tallepoosey river near to Emuckfau where our last battles were fought, and where we found the enemy enforted in a bend of the river, with a very strong breast work,—before we reached them, six miles, I was detached with 700. mounted men and 600 friendly Indians, to cross the river three miles below and take possession of the opposite side of the river, to prevent the enemy from crossing the river and escaping our army when attacked,—all our plans was executed to great advantage indeed—just as I had formed my men in line about ¼ of mile from the river, the cannon of our army in front commenced firing, and before one Indian crossed the river we had possession of the bank, the greater part of the enemy fought with savage fury while others of them ran in all directions, throwing themselves into the river and attempting to swim over, but not one escaped in that way—the battle commenced at half after ten in the morning, and continued untill night, our cannon played on their breast works near two hours, together with a great discharge of small arms,—when our men charged their walls by storm, which was done with great vigour, and suckcess, before we stormed their works, the friendly Indians had got in the rear of the enemy, which prevented them from flying back to their buildings, they stood the charge to admiration, and it was not unusual for the muzzles of the guns of both parties to meet in the port holes and both fire at the same time,—but the enemy was obliged to fly to the river, where all the remaining part that had not been killed, before, were shot in the water except a few that hid under the banks of the river, and which our men continued to find and kill untill it became to dark to see, perhaps 15 or 20, swam out that night which was all that escaped—the Slaughter was greater than all we had done before, we killed not less than 850, or 900, of them, and took about 500, squaws and children prisoners, we have now destroyed all the warriors of Tallepoosey—upper country—what will be our movements in the future I cannot say, the hickory ground is the next object, but how soon we cannot tell, our horses are worn down, and I fear will all dye, but we must go forwards at all costs,—I refer you to Capt. Smith for further particulars and news of our army—will only add, that things are quite different here to what they were in our former army, all is now content, no murmuring, to be heard—I don't know when I can return home, but don't expect to be long out—

With respects to yourself and family
I am with great regards
Your obt Servant
Jno. Coffee

N. B. Our loss in killed of white men was 26. and 106 wounded—of the friendly Indians 23 were killed and forty seven wounded—making our whole loss 49 killed and 153 wounded—

Lemuel Montgomery was killed in the charge against the breast works, by a ball through his head, after he reached the wall, he fired his pistol through a port hole, and killed an Indian and in an instant afterwards was shot through the same hole, and fell dead—never spoke,—

J. C.

Source: Tennessee Historical Society Miscellaneous Files, Box 3, c-118, Tennessee State Library and Archives.

VII. John Coffee to Andrew Jackson

Fort Williams 1st Apl. 1814
Maj. Genl. Andrew Jackson,

Sir,

Agreeably to your order of the 27th. Ultimo, I took up the line of march at half past six Oclock A.M. of the same day with a detachment of seven hundred cavalry and mounted gunmen and about six hundred Indians, five hundred of which were Cherokees and the balance friendly Creeks—I crossed the Tallepoosey river at the little Island ford about three miles below the bend, in which the enemy had concentrated, and then turned up the river bearing away from its clifts—when within half a mile of the village the savage yell was raised by the enemy, and I supposed he had discovered and was about to attack me. I immediately drew up my forces in line of battle in an open hilly woodland, and in that position moved on towards the yelling of the enemy—previous to this I had ordered the Indians on our approach to the bend of the river to advance secretly and take possession of the bank of the river and prevent the enemy from crossing on the approach of your army in his front—when within a quarter of a mile of the river, the firing of your Cannon commenced, when the Indians with me immediately rushed forward with great impetuosity to the river bank—my line was halted and kept in order of battle, expecting an attack on our rear from the Oakfuska villages, which lay down the river about eight miles below us—The firing of your Cannon and small arms in a short time became general and heavy, which animated our Indians, and seeing about one hundred of the Warriors and all the squaws and Children of the enemy running about among the huts of the Village, which was open to our view, they could no longer remain silent spectators, while some kept up a fire across the river (which is about one hundred & twenty yards wide) to prevent the enemy's approach to the bank, others plunged into the water and swam over the river for canoes that lay at the other shore in considerable numbers, and brought them over, in which Crafts a number of them embarked, and landed in the bend with the enemy—Colo. Gideon Morgan who commanded the Cherokees, Capt.[Hugh] Kerr, and Capt. William Russell, with a part of this company of Spies was amongst the first that crossed the river, they advanced into the Village and very soon drove the enemy from the huts up the River bank to the fortified works from which they were fighting you—they pursued and continued to annoy them during the whole action—This movement of my Indians forces left the river bank unguarded and made it necessary that I should send a part of my line to take possession of the river bank. I accordingly ordered about one third of the men to be posted around the bend on the river bank, whilst the balance remained in line to protect our rear—Captain Hammonds company of Raingers took post on the river bank on my right and during the whole engagement kept up a continued and destructive fire on those of the enemy that attempted to escape into the River and killed a very large proportion of those that were found dead under the bank above as well as many others sunk under water—I ordered Lieutenant Bean to take possession of the Island below with forty men, to prevent the enemy's taking refuge there, which was executed with promptitude, and which had a very happy effect, as many of the enemy did attempt their escape to the Island, but not one ever landed, they were sunk by Leut. Beans command ere they reached the bank—Attempts to cross the river at all points of the bend was made by the enemy, but not one escaped very few ever reached the bank, and that few was killed the instant they landed—From the report of my Officers as well as from my own observation, I feel warranted in saying that from Two hundred & fifty to three hundred of the enemy was buried under water and was not numbered with the dead that was found—My loss was two white men killed and ten wounded—and Twenty three friendly Indians killed and forty seven wounded—making in the whole of my detachment, Twenty five killed and fifty seven wounded—I left my position after you had gained possession of the bend and the enemy's works, and after the few who survived had taken shelter under the banks of the river, and marched up thro' the Newyorker Village, crossed over and joined the main army at seven Oclock P.M. during the action all the men and Officers of my detachment acted their several parts well—not one neglected to do the duty assigned to him with great firmness—Quarter Master [Joshua] Haskell attached himself to Capt Hammonds company, and fired not less than fifty rounds at the enemy during the course of the day and no doubt, done much execution.

I am Sir very respectfully
your very Humble Servant

Jno. Coffee
Brigd. Genl.

Source: Andrew Jackson Collection, 1788–1942, Tennessee State Library and Archives. This document appeared in several newspapers in the days following the battle and has been published in Harold D. Moser et al., eds., *The Papers of Andrew Jackson*, vol. 3: *1814–1815* (Knoxville: University of Tennessee Press), 55–57. The original can be viewed online at the Tennessee Virtual Archive website.

VIII. John Coffee to his wife, Mary Donelson Coffee, at Jefferson, Rutherford County, Tennessee

Fort Williams 1st. April 1814

My Dear,

I have to announce to you one other victory obtained over our enemy, at the same bend of the Tallepoosey, near where we fought our last battles, we attacked the enemy, on the 27th. of last month, the enemy were about one thousand in number, enforted in abend of the river, with very strong works, I crossed the river with 700, mounted men and 600. Indians and took possession of the other bank to prevent them swiming over the river and escaping—all was executed well, the enemy fought with their usual desperation, but we overpowered them, and after Cannonading them about two hours, we charged their works by storm, and put the whole to death but a few that hid under the banks of the river, the slaughter was great we counted 557 dead bodies on the ground besides about 300. that was shot and sunk in the river, making in the whole that we killed from 850. to 900,—and took about 500 prisoners. Squaws and children—we lost on our part of white men 26 killed and 106. wounded besides 23 friendly Indians killed and 47. wounded—this place was an assemblage of all the upper towns on the Tallapoosey, and which we have now destroyed, it only remains that we take possession of the forks of the river and fight one battle there, to finish the Creek war—this I hope we will do in ten days from this time—I cannot say precisely when I shall be discharged but think it will be less than one month from this time—I have never heard from you since I left home, only by a letter recd. from Col [Robert] Hays,[9] he says you are well, cannot you write me, having now nearly completed our business here, I shall soon turn me towards home when I hope to enjoy the remainder of my life with you in quiet—my love to our little daughter—and all friends—farewell—

Jno. Coffee

Lemul Montgomery was killed in battle at the charge against the breast works, by a ball through the head.—JC

Source: Tennessee Historical Society/Tennessee State Library and Archives, Dyas Collection of John Coffee Papers, Accession # : 38, Box 3, Folder 18. The original document can be viewed online at the Tennessee Virtual Archive website. For the entire collection of letters from Coffee to his wife, see "Letters of General John Coffee to His Wife, 1812–1815," *Tennessee Historical Magazine* 2 (December 1916): 264–95.

IX. John Donelson to his father, Captain John Donelson, Davidson County, Tennessee[10]

Fort Williams April 1st. 1814

Dear Father

We returned to this place yesterday after an excursion of eight days up the Tallapoosy, we were up fifty two miles from this to the bend of the Tallapoosy where we were in January. The Indian name of the place I believe is Tehoopky, which was fortified in a most military manner and by far surpassed any of our expectations. The Fort was maned with between eight hundred and a thousand warriors, we attacked the fort on the morning of the 27th. of March at half past ten the action raged with considerable warmth for about five hours the enemy at length gave way in every direction and numbers attempted to cross the river but Genl. Coffee's Brigade had crossed at a ford about two miles below the Fort and completely taken possession of the other Bank which prevented them from making their escapes by crossing the river, hundreds of them were killed in attempting to swim the river; Their defeat was total, our cannon had no effect upon their fortification, we were compeled to take it by storm. Major Montgomery fell gallantly chargeing at the head of his men, he was shot in the head—Our loss in whites and Indians does not exceed fifty killed and a proportionable number wounded, a more brilliant victory was never before obtained than that of the battle of Tehoopky give my compliments to Aunt [Mary] Caffery and tell her that Jacky [John Caffery Jr.][11] is well he has attached himself to our company

I am your affectionate son
John Donelson Jr

Source: Tennessee State Historical Society/Tennessee State Library and Archives, T-100, Misc. Collection.

X. Andrew Jackson to Rachel Jackson

Head quarters Fort Williams
April 1rst. 1814

My Dear,

I returned to this place on yesterday three oclock P.M. from an excursion against Tohopeka, and about one hour after had the pleasure of receiving your affectionate letter of the 22nd ultimo—

I have the pleasure to state to you that on the 27th. March that I attacked & have destroyed the whole combined force, of the Newyokas [New Yauka], oakfuska, [Okfuskee], Hillabays [Hillabee], Fish ponds, ocaias [Okchai], and ufalee [Eufaula], Tribes—The *carnage* was *dreadfull*—They had possessed themselves of one of the most military sites, I Ever saw, which they had as strongly fortified with logs, across the neck of a bend—I endeavored, to levell the works with my cannon, but in vain—The balls passed thro the works without shaking the wall—but carrying destruction to the enemy behind it—I had sent Genl Coffee across the river, with his horse and Indians who had compleatly surrounded the bend—which cut off their escape—and the cherokees Effected a landing on the extreme point of the bend with about one hundred and fifty of Genls coffees Brigade, including Capt [William Russell] Russles spy company—The Battle raged, about two hours, when I found those engaged in the interior of the bend, were about to be overpowered, I ordered, the charge and carried the works, by storm—after which they Indians took posesesion of the river bank, and part of their works raised with brush getting into the interior of the bend—and It was dark before we finished killing them—I ordered the dead bodies of the Indians to be counted, the next morning, and exclusive of those buried in their watry grave, who were killed in the [river] and who after being wounded plunged into it, there were counted, five hundred and fifty seven—from the report of Genl Coffee and the officers surrounding the bend, they are of oppinion, that there could not be less than three hundred, killed in the river, who sunk and could not be counted—I have no doubt, but at least Eight hundred and fifty were slain—about twenty who had hid under the bank in the water, made their Escape in the night, one of whom was taken the next morning who gives this account, that they were all wounded from which I believe about 19 wounded Indians alone escaped—we took about three hundred and fifty prisoners, weomen & children and three warriors—What effect this will produce upon those infatuated and deluded people I cannot yet say—having destroyed at To.hope.ka, three of the principal prophets leaving but two in their nation—having tread their holy ground as they termed it, and destroyed all their chiefs & warriors on the Tallapoosee river above the big bend, it is probable they may now sue for peace should they not (If I can be supplied with provisions) I will give them, with the permission of heaven the final stroke at the hickory ground, in a few days we have lost in killed of the whites 26, and one hundred and seven wounded—amonghst the former is Major [Lemuel] Montgomery who bravely fell on the walls, and of the latter Colo. [William] Carroll—slightly—our friends all safe, and Jack you may say to Mrs. Caffery reallised all my expectations he fought bravely—and killed an Indian—every officer and man did his duty—the 39th distinguished themselves and so did the militia, who stormed the works with them. There never was more heroism or roman courage displayed—I write in haste surrounded with a pressure of business, and a little fatigued—I will write you again before I leave this place—for the present I can only add, that I hope shortly to put an end to the war and return to your arms, kiss my little andrew[12] for me, tell him I have a warriors bow & quiver for him—give my compliments to all friends, and cheer up the spirits of your Sister Cafferry—and receive my sincere prayers for your health & happiness untill I return—affectionately adieu—

Andrew Jackson

Source: Andrew Jackson Papers: Series 1, General Correspondence and Related Items, 1775–1885, Library of Congress, Manuscript Division. Printed in Harold D. Moser et al., eds., *The Papers of Andrew Jackson*, vol. 3: *1814–1815*, 54–55.

XI. "Extract of a letter from Major Gen. Jackson to Col. [Peter] Perkins[13] . . ."

HEAD-QUARTERS, Fort Williams, April 1, 1814

Sir__I have been so surrounded with the pressure of business since my return from the excursion to the Tallaposie, that I had not time to write. I have now only a moment—The 27th in the morning was the day I reached the strong hold—I had detached Gen. [John] Coffee with his brigade in the morning of the 27th, with about 500 Cherokees & friendly Creeks, to cross the river below them, and form a circle around the bend in which stood their fortification. I reached Tohopeca half after ten, A.M. and was hailed with a challenge to the combat from their strong wall. The cannon, under the direction of Capt. [William] Bradford, chief engineer, was directed to open a brisk fire upon their wall; at a distance of about 200 yards on our left, and one hundred yards on our right. At this moment I was advised Gen. Coffee was at his post, from a height. The order was immediately put into execution, and notwithstanding every shot penetrated the fortress and carried with it death and destruction; still such was the strength of the wall that it never shook. After firing about 70 rounds at it, and finding the

Cherokees, Capt. [William] Russell's spies, and a number of Gen. Coffee's brigade had effected a landing, & had attacked the enemy on the rear—finding that the Creeks beat them back and our friends were suffering—I determined to storm their works—At half after 12 o'clock the order was given, the long roll beat, and the works carried.—never was more bravery displayed—every officer done his duty—the 39th Regiment led on by the gallant Col. [John] Williams and Maj. [Lemuel] Montgomery, in the centre; the right, by the gallant Col. [Samuel] Bunch; the advanced guard who had been formed on the right of the artillery, by the brave Col. [James W.] Sit[t]ler; the left by Capt. [John] Gordon of the spies, and Capt. Murry of Gen. [Thomas] Johnson's Brigade. All distinguished themselves—Capt. [Thomas] Camp, acting deputy quarter-master, and col. [William] Carroll, Inspector General, went with the foremost; and James Lewis of the artillery, although wounded, was amongst the foremost—In fact it was difficult to detain the artillery men at their posts, although 10 had been previously wounded. The carnage was dreadful—557 bodies were counted of the enemy on the field, three hundred is supposed to have sunk in the river, killed by the surroudding cavalry and Indians, who shot them attempting to make their escape across the river; making in all 857 killed—our loss 26 killed, 107 wounded—the Creeks and Cherokees loss 23 killed and 47 wounded, in all 203. The communication is open between me and Georgia. There was about 350 prisoners taken, some of whom is carried by Maj. [William] M'Intosh to the Big Warrior,[14] many taken off by the Cherokees and the balance taken by the friendly Creeks I send you for safe keeping—you will keep them together in the neighborhood of Huntsville, or in the town, until further ordered, and call on the contractor for provisions for them—you will cause them to be humanely treated.

Source: The letter was originally published in the *Madison Gazette* (Huntsville, Alabama) and reprinted on April, 27, 1814, in the *Nashville Whig*, the source of this transcription.

XII. Alexander McCulloch to Frances McCulloch

Fort Williams Apl. 1st 1813 [1814]

My Dear Wife

On Sunday last the 27th. of March the Red Sticks paid severly for their folly in waging war against the whites by a loss of at least 800 of their Warriors which lay dead on the field of Battle. The whole army under the command of Genl. [Andrew] Jackson sett out from this post on the Coosa River 60 miles below Fort Strother on the 23rd. to march against the enemy's fort in the bend of the Tallapoosa River distance 52½ miles and when having gotten within 6 miles of the Fort Genl. [John] Coffee's Brigade was detached across the Tallapoosa crossing 2½ miles below in order to prevent their making their escape by swimming the River or by canoes of which they had at least 100. The Indians Cherokees and friendly Creeks accompanied us and immediately swam across the river and brought over their canoes and carried over their warriors and commenced a fire on them under their breast work in the rear which very soon put a part of them to flight who were killed by our men in swimming the River, the Tallapoosa might be truly called a River of blood for the water was so stained that at 10 Oclock at night it was very perceptably bloody so much so that it could not be used. The battle commenced at 10 Oclock A.M. and continued with a tremendous fire for five hours and did not end till at least 10 Oclock at night and then leaving a balance of 16 wounded that had taken refuge under the banks who were killed the next morning. A number of very good judges say that there was 1000 Warriors and if so there were more killed that I have stated for there was not more than 30 that did escape & that was by secriting themselves under the banks amongst brush & swimming the River in the night most all of which a prisoner which we took says was wounded. I enclose you a plan of the bend of the River together with the fortifications and situations of both the Infantry & cavalry. There was only 25 of the whites killed on the ground and 106 wounded a number of which have since died but in all not more than 40 among them but two of your acq[uaintance] which was [Adam?] Shipley & Maj. Lemuel Montgomery who no[bly died] at the enemy's fortifications waving his hat an [huzzai]ng when he received a ball in the head which instantly killed him—My Dear it is not in my power to say when I [will be] able to reach home but rest assured that nothing [missing section] one moment, take care of yourself & the children w[hen] oportunity offers in a few days write me otherwise y[ou may]] let it alone as we will be obliged to return on [account] of our horses which are nearly exhausted by famine.

I am Dr Fransey
Yr affectionate & loving
Alexr. McCulloch

N.B. Joe engaged in the fighting and discharged 4 shots at the enemy—

Source: McCulloch Papers, University of Texas. For additional information, see Thomas W. Cutrer, "'The Tallapoosa Might Truly Be Called the [*sic*] River of Blood': Major Alexander McCulloch and the Battle of Horseshoe Bend, March 27, 1813 [*sic*]," *Alabama Review* 43(January 1990): 35–39.

XIII. "Copy of a letter from Colonel Gideon Morgan, commander of the Cherokees, to William G. Blount, esq dated Fort Williams, April 1, 1814"

You have been informed of our departure from Fort Strother, and arrival at this place on the 21st of March, on the 24th Gen. Jackson took up his line of march for Tohopiska or fortified town on the Talapoosee, commonly called the horse-shoe—on the evening of the 29th [26th] he encamped about six miles north west of it. the army next morning was divided into two divisions. The horse and Indians commanded by Gen. [John] Coffee, crossed the river two miles below the town, with directions to line the bank in the whole extent of the bend, by the Cherokees and friendly Creeks—while the horse acted as a guard on the high ground, to defend our rear from an attack from the Oakfuskee Indians, who were expected from below.—This precaution was however unnecessary as their whole force had been concentrated the day before. Gen. Coffee had arrived on the opposite shore, about half a mile below the town, when Gen. Jackson's approach before the fortification was announced by the discharge of artillery, and in quick succession that of a brigade of infantry. The Cherokees immediately rushed to the point assigned them, which they did in regular order, and in a manner honorable to themselves, that is the bend was in no place left vacant, and those fugitives who had taken to flight, fell an easy prey to their vengeance.—The draft which Lieutenant Rice encloses, will give you a better description of the place than I can, to which I refer you. The breast work was composed of five large logs, with two ranges of port holes well put together, artillery had no effect more than to bore it whenever it struck; nature had done much, but when completed by art the place was formidable indeed, the high ground which extended about mid-way from the breast work to the river was in some manner open, but the declivity & flat which surrounded it was filled with fallen timber, the growth of which was very heavy, and had been so arranged that every tree afforded them a breast work, forming a communication or cover to the next, and so on to the river bank, in which caverns had been dug for their security, and our annoyance. The breast work in its whole extent was lined by savages, made desperate from their situation. The 39th was drawn up on the left in a line extending from the center to the river bank, the right was occupied by the militia. The artillery on an eminence 200 yards in rear of the breast work, on which it kept up a steady and well directed fire, though without effect—in this manner the battle became stationary for some time, say one hour, when the Cherokees crossed the river by swimming and brought from the opposite shore a number of canoes, in which they crossed under cover of the town, and their own guns; they halted under cover of the bank, and the canoes were sent back for a reinforcement.—Understanding General Jackson was about charging the breast works in its whole extent, I rode with all possible dispatch to inform Major [Lemuel] Montgomery who commanded the left of the 39th on the river above. On my return about 150 or 200 Cherokees had crossed, and were warmly engaged with the hostile Creeks. I then crossed with Major [John] Walker[15] and 30 others and ascended the high ground which the Cherokees were then in possession of, we were here warmly assailed on every quarter except our rear, w[h]ere we only kept open by the dint of hard fighting. The Cherokees were continually crossing and our numbers increased in about the proportion in which the Creeks were diminished who laid prostrate in every quarter—their numbers were vastly superior to ours, but were occupied in maintaining their breast work, which they appeared determined never to surrender; about one hour after my arrival on the summit, I received a wound in the right side of my head, which had like to have terminated my existence, I however in a short time recovered and heard the heavenly intelligence that the 39th had charged and were then in possession of the breast works, this was an arduous undertaking, and the cool deliberate manner in which it was effected, reflects the highest credit on this bulwark of our army. I shall not attempt a description—in the detailed official account justice will no doubt be done them. The fight commenced 17 minutes after 10 and continued without intermission until dark—next morning some were killed, who it appears were determined never to quit their enchanted ground.—On counting their dead 557 were found on the field, many I know perished in crossing, and numbers were sunk in the river, the whole loss in killed could not be less than 7 or 800. The loss of the 39th 72 killed and wounded. Major Montgomery, Lieut. Sommerville and Lieut. Moulton were among the former. The loss of the Cherokees, 18 killed and 35 wounded, many badly. The Cherokees have been permitted to return to their homes.

Source: Letter originally printed in the *Clarion and Tennessee State Gazette,* Nashville, Tennessee, Tuesday, April 12, 1814.

XIV. John Reid to Betsy Reid, April 1, 1814

Ft. Williams 1st April 1814

Dear Betsy,

I have only time to inform you that I have returned in safety from our expedition to the Tallapoosa, where on the 27th. ult, we gained the most signal victory that has ever been obtained over Indians. Advised of our approach they had gathered in from six or eight towns to the number, it is said by the prisoners, of a thousand. We found them in the same bend where they were encamped when they came out, & attacked us on the morning of 22d. January. Across the point of land along which we must approach them, they had extended a breastwork, from five to eight feet high, of large pine logs fitted in with greater skill & strength, by far, than any I have ever witnessed. It was of such a form that you could only approach it by being exposed to a double & cross fire, from the enemy who lay concealed & in security behind it. At half past ten Oclk A. M. we planted our cannon, on an eminence distant from its nearest corner about eighty yards & from its farthest about 250. For two hours we laboured, to batter it down, or make a breach in it; but our efforts were unavailing. Our balls only passed through, killing some behind it, but doing no material injury to the works. All this while we kept up a brisk fire upon such of the enemy as shewed themselves behind the wall or endeavored to approach it from the town, which was situated at the lower extremity of the peninsula. In the meantime our men were receiving frequent wounds, & some of them their deaths, from the balls which were fired through the port holes. At this juncture, a part of the Cherokees, & Capt. [William] Russells company of Spies, who had crossed the river below with Genl. [John] Coffee in order to surround the enemy so that none of them should escape, anxious to participate in the battle crossed over in canoes, to the town, & set fire to a few of the houses. That being done, they advanced towards the breastworks, & commenced firing on the enemy who lay behind them. It was soon discovered however, that this diversion could not dislodge them; and indeed the enemy were very well defended by logs on the inner side also. The general now determined to take possession of the works by storm; & every man hailed the order for a charge with acclamation. This was a moment of feeling & not of reflection. I never had such emotions as while the long roll was beating, & the troops in motion. It was not fear, it was not anxiety or concern of the fate of those who were so soon to fall but it was a kind of enthusiasm that thrilled through every nerve & animated me with the belief that they day was ours, without adverting to what it must cost us. In a little while my hopes were realized. Our troops, not to be dismayed by the fall of their

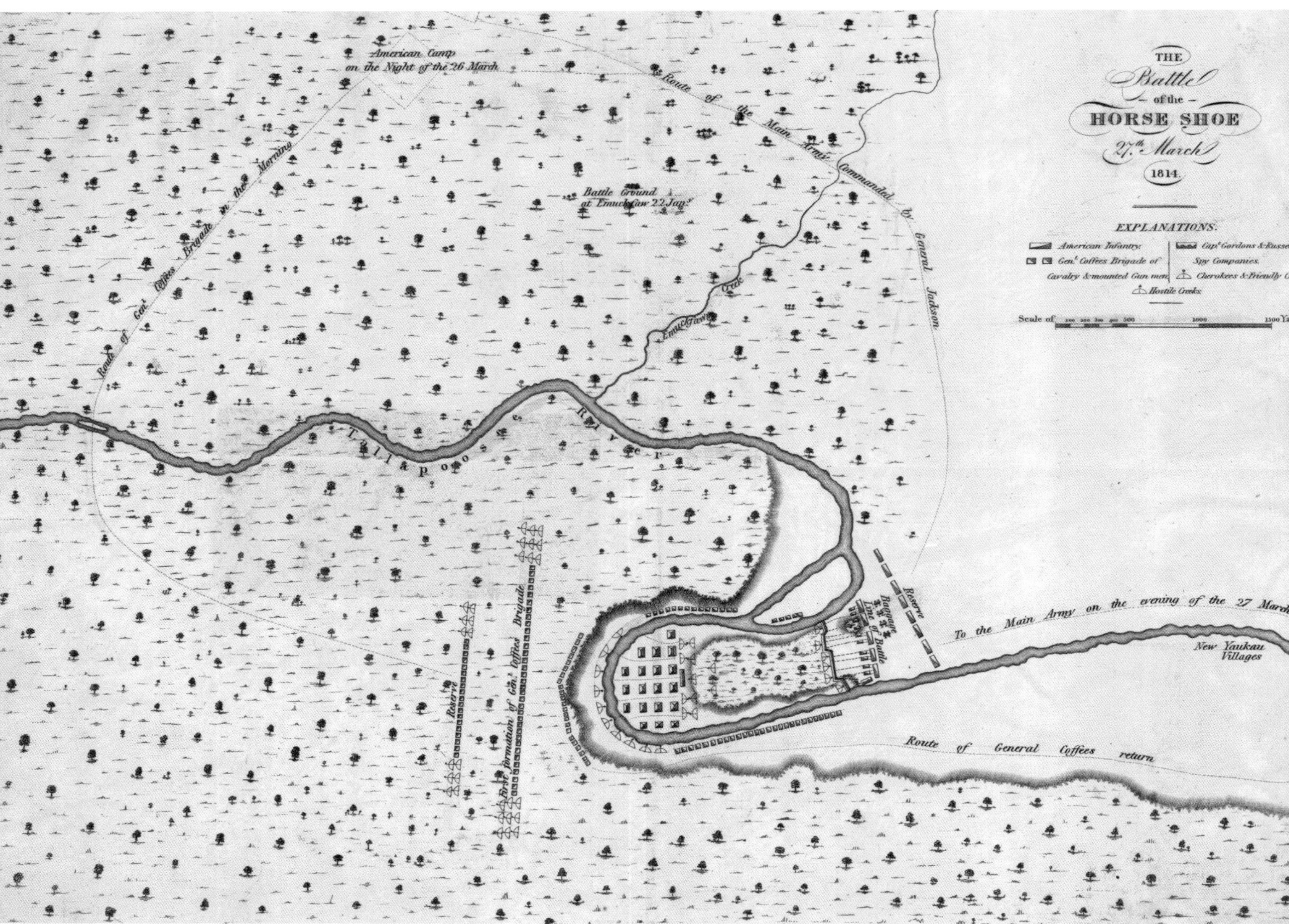

FIGURE 38. *The Battle of the Horse Shoe 27th March 1814*. One of the most widely distributed maps, copied from a version of Major Cheatham's map, appeared in *The Life of Andrew Jackson*, published in 1817. The work was begun by John Reid, who served as Jackson's aide-de-camp during the war, and completed by John Henry Eaton after Reid's death in 1816. Courtesy of the Birmingham Public Library.

officers, several of whom were shot down as they advanced, took posession of the nearer side of the wall. We were now fighting, muzzle to muzzle through the same port holes. We at length mounted the wall & took possesion of the other side,—Then commenced the work of death, in all of its most gloomy features. The enemy fought with the bravery of desperation; but at length were cut to pieces. Five hundred & fifty seven were killed on the land; & a great many more on the water, endeavouring to escape—by Genl. Coffee's men on the other side. Their prophet Monahoee was killed by a grape shot in the mouth—a very appropriate punishment for his impostures. Our loss including the Indians, may be about fifty killed & 150 wounded—many of them mortally. I lament the loss of poor Major [Lemuel] Montgomery who was shot dead at the wall—having just killed an Indian through a port hole with his pistol.

In a few days we shall take up the line of march for the Hickory ground, with a force greatly diminished by death, sickness, & discharges. There we shall have to fight the remaining force of the nation; and there I hope Heaven will again prosper our arms.

I am very anxious to get home; & the general thinks it will not be long before we all return.

Kiss the children & believe me to be affectionately yours,
John Reid

Source: John Reid Papers, Library of Congress.

XV. John Coffee to his wife, Mary Donelson Coffee, at Jefferson, Rutherford County, Tennessee

Fort Williams 2nd. April 1814

My Dear,

I wrote you yesterday by Mr. [William B.] Lewis[16] who was the bearer of an express from Genl. Jackson, he promised to leave the letter at Murfreesbrough, from where I know you will get it, but Mr. Wm. [William] White is going to start this moment and is going so near you, I drop this line by him,—in my other I give you an account of an other battle we have had, in which we killed from eight hundred to nine hundred of the enemy, and took about 500. prisoners—this is the greatest defeat we have ever given them, we killed three of their prophets in this battle one of whom was a very principal one, this will damp them very much—I herewith send you a plat of the river and bend, where we fought for you satisfaction to see our movements, I expect the day after tomorrow we will start to the hickory ground and will reach that point in 3 or 4 days, perhaps we may have one battle more, in that quarter before they give up their country, but they cannot hold out, they are already nearly starved, to death, having eat up all their provisions—as I mentioned in my last I do not know when I will be at home, but suppose one month will finish all my duties—Say to Polley Harris that I have not seen Simpson since I come out only met him in the road and talked about fifteen minutes he was appointed in the quarter master department and remained in Madison, where I suppose he is now—

I hope our little farm is going on well, I engaged with Robt. Warnock to carry some cotton seed from Madison County for you, I fear he has not done it if they should come, I wish them planted even if it should be late,—how is Mr. & Mrs. Eastin, make my respects to them,—love to you and Mary

Farewell my dear
Jno. Coffee

Source: Tennessee Historical Society/Tennessee State Library and Archives, Dyas Collection of John Coffee Papers, Accession # : 38, Box 3, Folder 13. The original document may be viewed online at the Tennessee Virtual Archive website.

XVI. Captain William Bradford to Major General William H. Harrison

Fort Williams Coosee river April 5th, 1814

Maj. Genl. Wm H. Harrison
Dear Sir,

You have no doubt heard of the last battle fought by Maj. Genl. [Andrew] Jackson—against the Creek Indians—at the fortified bend of the Tallepoosee river by them thought invulnerable—The particulars of the battle you will, no doubt have seen, ere this in Genl. Jackson's official communication on this subject—

Believing that a map of that part of the river occupied by the savages, together with Genl. Jackson order of the line of march will not be unacceptable to you, I have the honor to enclose them to you—

From what I can learn, the Genl. has had to encounter many difficultis, during his present campaign against the Creek Indians—It would be unnecessary to name to you sir, any of them, your own feelings have tested in a similar way.

After returning from the battle on Tallepoosee, the Genl. began to make preparations for to set out to Hoithlewauli a considerable village on the Tallepoosee river when it is supposed, that most of the shattered remains of the enimy are collected, from that point he will go immediately to the junction of the Coosee and Tallepoosee, the only point at which we can learn that any of the enimy remains—

The success of Genl. Jackson under all circumstances are without a parallel—I had thought, that the numbers killed in former battles had been exagerated but I cannot be mistaken in what passes before my own eyes—That 557 Indians were found dead on the ground is a fact and that the river was red with blood from the number that was killed in it is equally true—I never witnessed such carnage, the Creeks fought with all the fury of the northern Indians—I came to this army by order of Col. Wm P. Anderson of the 24th. Infty—I am unable as yet to undergo the fatigues of a march or do duty on foot—The Genl. however has been pleased to appoint me principal Engineer. I superintended the firing of two pieces of artillery at the last battle, and altho I had the pleasure of killing many of them yet so strong was their breast work, that I could not make a breach in it. it was built with all the military skills the ground would afford—

The police of the Genls. camp is good—The militia are equaly subordinate with the regular troops They must do their duty—one was shot not long ago for mutiny—

As it is expected that the present campaign will terminate shortly—I beg you will order me to join you before you commence operations again in the north.

Your name is frequently mentioned in this army and always in terms of respect—The Genl. speaks of you as a military man in respectful terms—

After we have completed the work at the before mentioned points, I will again do myself the honor of addressing you—giving you some particulars of the excursion—

I shall thank you to write me if convenient at any time

I have the honor to be very Respectfully yr M Obt Servt
Wm Bradford
17th Regt U S Inf

Source: William Henry Harrison Papers: Series 1, General Correspondence, 1734–1939, Library of Congress, Manuscript Division.

XVII. Report of Andrew Jackson [to General Thomas Pinckney], April 5, 1814

Ft. Williams
5, April 1814.

Sir,

By Maj. [William] McIntosh the Coweta, I forwarded you on the 28th ult. from the battle ground near New-Yauka, a hasty account of the incidents and result of my expedition to the Tallapoosie. As a more circumstantial detail is usual, and may be expected, I undertake to give it; altho' I have now but little more leisure than I had then.—

Leaving a sufficient force for the defence of this place, and to scour the surrounding country, I took up the line of march with the remainder of my forces, on the 24th ult. taking with me eight days rations. Having opened a passage over the ridge which divided the waters of the Coosee and Tallapoosie, I encamped on the night of the 26th ult. within six miles of a bend of the Tallapoosie, in which the warriors from Oakfuska, Oakchoya, New-Yauca, Hillebees, Fishpond, and Eufaula towns, appraised of my approach, had collected to meet me. This bend which resembles in its curvature that of a horse-shoe includes I conjecture, eighty or a hundred acres. The river immediately around it, is deep, and somewhat upwards of 100 yards wide.

As a situation for defense it was selected with judgement, and improved with great industry and art. Across the neck of land which leads to it, they had erected a breastwork eighty poles[17] in length, from five to eight feet high, and of remarkable compactness and strength. Prepared with double rows of portholes, well formed and skillfully arranged, it was of such a figure, that an army could not approach it, without being exposed to a cross fire. The exact numbers of warriors here assembled cannot be known, it is said by the prisoners to have been a thousand—one thing appears certain, that relying upon their strength and their situation, they calculated upon repelling us with ease.—

Early on the morning of the 27th, I detached Gen. [John] Coffee with 700 Cavalry and mounted gun-men, & 600 Indians to cross the river three miles below, and surround the bend in such a manner, that none of them should escape. With the remainder of the forces I proceeded in order, along the point of land which led to the front of the breast-work and at half past ten o'clock A.M. I had formed my line of battle across the straight, and planted my artillery on an eminence about eighty yards from the nearest part of the wall, and about three hundred from the farthest. From this point I immediately opened a brisk fire upon its centre; but altho' the balls which passed through, killed several of the enemy, they were not dispersed, nor was any important damage done to the works.

The small arms in the meantime, were actively employed against such of the enemy as shewed themselves beyond the wall by changing their position, or venturing to approach it from the interior or from the town situated at the bottom of the peninsula. This was continued with a few short intermissions for two hours; when capt. [William] Russells company of spies, and a part of the Cherokee force, conducted by Col. [Gideon] Morgan, obtained canoes and crossed over the lower extremity of the bend—setting fire to a few of the buildings, as a signal to us of their arrival, they hastened, with great gallantry afterwards towards the breastwork, and opened a fire on the enemy who lay behind it. This was returned and spiritedly kept up for fifteen minutes; when it became obvious that the enemy were not to be enticed or driven by it from their posts. This consideration together with the knowledge that Gen. Coffee had now completely occupied the opposite banks of the river, determined me to take possession of their works by storm. There seemed no other means left, of bringing the conflict to a speedy and successful termination.

It was very fortunate, that the men by whom I was to undertake this measure wished for nothing more anxiously. The Regulars and Militia manifested and equal solicitude for the enterprize, and equally distinguished themselves in the execution of it. The effect corresponded with the favorable passage with which it was undertaken. In a little while we were in possession of the nearer side of the wall; when a severe conflict was maintained for several minutes, through the same port holes. Many of the balls of the enemy were found, welded to the muzzles of our guns. At length we mounted the wall, and gained possession of the opposite side. The most obstinate and bloody contest now ensued. The enemy resolved not to yield, and forseeing the doom which awaited them, fought with that kind of bravery which desperation inspires;—but the result was no longer doubtful. Intelligent bravery triumphed over savage ferocity; and the enemy every where repulsed, were slaughtered in heaps. Five hundred and fifty seven were left dead on the peninsula; besides many who, during the continuance of the action, were thrown into the river by their surviving friends, and many, who endeavoring to escape were killed in it, by Gen. Coffee's men, from the opposite banks. Their loss in killed, it is believed has not fallen short of eight hundred.

The number that escaped by secreting themselves under the banks of the river, I learn by prisoners taken the next day, did not exceed twenty; most of whom were wounded.

Three or four women and children who had mixed with the men were unfortunately killed by accident.

The prisoners, whose number is not accurately known, have been sent to Talladega by the friendly Creeks—They are all women and children except three or four, and exceed three hundred.

Our loss in whitemen were 26 killed and 105 wounded, in cherokees 18 killed and 36 wounded, and in friendly Creeks 5 killed and eleven wounded:—a small number, when we consider the nature of the conflict and the loss of the enemy.

Several of our wounded have died since the battle.

In making their charge, the 39th Reg't. U.S. Infantry was led on by their skillful and intrepid commander Col. [John] Williams, and by the gallant Major [Lemuel] Montgomery who fell at the wall, the advance guard by the Agt. Gen. Col. [James W.] Sittler; a company of spies by capt. [John] Gordon; and a few Companies of Gen. [George] Doherty's Brigade of East Tennessee Militia, by Col. [Samuel] Bunch. Col. [John A.] Cheatham's & [Stephen] Copeland's Regt's. of West Tennessee Militia, were stationed as a reserve behind the baggage and ammunition waggons; and although they were not brought into the engagement, I have the utmost confidence, they would have acted meritoriously if they had been.

The Artillery company commanded by capt. [Joel] Parrish behaved with their usual gallantry—Ten of them were wounded, and one killed. Capt. Wm. Bradford of the 17th Reg't. U.S. Infantry, who superintended the firing of the cannon acted with great skill and bravery; and has entitled himself to the expression of my thanks.

The battle continued to rage until three o'clock P.M.: but the carnage did not cease, till an end was put to it by the darkness of the night.

The loss we sustained in storming the breastwork, was less than we could have expected. if it were not known that in fighting Indians, a bold charge conduces not less to the safety of the assailants, than to the certainty of victory.

It would be tedious to specify particular instances of meritorious conduct; and indeed it would be hardly proper, where all acted so praise-worthy. I had a fair opportunity of observing; and I did not witness a single individual who failed or hesitated in the performance of his duty. I may say I have seen the rare instance of a battle in which nothing was done amiss, and to which it was not easy to suggest any amendment, after it was done.

I enclose you a plan somewhat more correct than that which I forwarded you from the battle-ground. I also send a copy of Gen. Coffee's brigade report.

Andrew Jackson
Major General

Source: Published in the *Nashville Whig*, Wednesday, May 24, 1814.

XVIII. John Reid to his father, April 5, 1814

Ft Williams 5th April 1814

Dear Father

On the 17th of last month we commenced the line of march from Ft Strother; & reached this place, distant from it 59 miles, on the morning of 21st. The boats with the provisions arrived the next day,—having met with many difficulties in the navigation. At this place we immediately commenced building a depot for supplies; but it is not yet completed.

Having made the necessary arrangements, & left a sufficient force for the defence of this place, & to scour the surrounding country we set out on the morning of the 24th. for the Tallapoosee. The enemy, from various towns, had collected in a bend of this river, (resembling a horse-shoe in its form), to welcome our arrival. You can scarcely imagine a situation stronger by nature, or rendered more secure by art. Across the neck of land which led into it, they had erected a breast-work, from five to eight feet high, of the utmost compactness & strength; & prepared with double rows of port-holes, very skillfully arranged. It was impossible, from the zigzag form of the wall, to approach it without being exposd to a double & cross fire; or to rake it to any advantage with the cannon even if you had had possession of one of its extremities.

The area of this bend, thus bounded by the wall & by the river, included about a hundred acres; & the number of the warriors therein collected is said & believed to have been about a thousand.

On the morning of the 27th (having encamped the night before about six miles from the place) Genl. [John] Coffee was detached with all the horsemen & Indian force to cross the river at a ford about three miles below their encampment, & to surround the bend in such a manner that none of them should escape. With the remainder of the force we marched slowly & in order, along the point of land which led to the front of the breast-work; & at half past ten Oclk our battle line was formed, & our artillery planted on a small eminence, about 80 yards distant from the nearest part of the works & about 250 from the farthest. From this position a brisk fire was immediately opened, from a six & a three pounder, upon the centre of the wall; but it had no effect to demolish it, or to drive the enemy from behind it, altho many of them were killed by the balls which pased through. With the rifles & musquetry we kept up a galling fire wherever the enemy (as they oftentimes did) shewed themselves beyond the works, or returned to approach them. This was continued, with a few short intermissions, for about two hours; during all which time we were exposed to the shot of the enemy—many of which took effect.

It was at this juncture that a company of spies & a part of the Cherokee force who accompanied Genl. Coffee, impatient to participate in the battle, crossed over the river in canoes, to the lower extremity of the bend, & set fire to a few of the houses which were there situated. Having done this they immediately advanced towards the breastwork, & opened a fire upon the enemy who lay behind it.

It was not long however before we discovered that this force was wholly insufficient to divert the enemy or dislodge them from their posts; & Genl. Coffee having completely occupied the opposite banks of the river, Genl. [Andrew] Jackson, now determined upon taking possession of the works by storm. Never were men, in all the world, more impatient for a charge than those by whom it was now to be made. The regulars & militia were equally anxious, & equally distinguished themselves. The least deliberation must have convinced every one that many must fall in their perilous undertaking; but no one deliberated. It was, in truth, a moment of feeling, & not of reflection. The long-roll was sounded, & the charge made. In a little while we were in possession of the nearer side of the works; & here a terrible conflict ensued, through the same portholes. In many instances the balls of the enemy were found welded to the muzzles of our guns. At length we mounted the walls, & took possession of the other side. Now it was that the contest was not so much for victory as for life. On every side were heard the groans of the dying & the shouts of the victors. The enemy were completely routed, & cut to pieces; but most of them fought to the last with all the fury of desperation.

Five hundred & fifty seven were left dead on the peninsula; besides many who were thrown into the river by their surviving friends & many who were killed from the opposite side of the river in attempting to escape. Their loss in killed, cannot have been less than 800; & must have been greater if their original number was a thousand, as the prisoners state it to have been. It is certain that not more than twenty can have escaped.

The number of prisoners is not exactly known, but is exceeds three hundred—all women & children, except three or four.

Our loss was forty nine killed on the spot, & a hundred & fifty four wounded, of whom many have since died—

Among the dead of the enemy was found their famous prophet, Monahoee, struck in the mouth with a grape-shot; as if heaven directed an appropriate punishment for his impostures & lies. Two other prophets were also killed—leaving no others on the Tallapoosa.

The battle raged for five hours; but the carnage did not cease, until it was suspended by the darkness of the night. The next morning it was resumed, & sixteen of the enemy killed who had secreted themselves under the banks, & remained there all night.

On the 28th. we commenced our return march for this place, which we reached on the 31st—a distance of 52½ miles.

With a force greatly diminished by sickness, death & discharges, we shall set out in a few days, for the Hickory Ground to meet a greater force of the enemy, than any we have yet encountered. There their last hopes are anchored, & there, I trust Heaven has doomed them to perish. The conflict I know, will be severe; but I rely upon the bravery of our troops, the skill of our commander, & the justice of our cause.

I wish the war were at an end; and I long anxiously to be at home, & in peace.

I enjoy good health; tho sickness prevails very much in our Camp.

Remember me to my mother & the children
I am affectionably
yr son
John Reid

Source: John Reid Papers, Library of Congress, Manuscript Division.

XIX. Jesse Webb[18] to Judge McNairy, October 28, 1817, in regard to his application for a pension

Brazewell, Claiborne County Tennessee
October 28th 1817
Sir

I am informed that Invalids of this State must apply through you to obtain their pension. I served three years under General [Anthony] Wayne between fort Erie and fort Detroit principally and at the defeat of the Indians on the Auglaize was wounded in the right thigh above the knee but as it did not injure me much I made no account of it.[19]

Being 45 years of age I volunteered to support Gen. [Andrew] Jackson in the fall of 1814[1813] but being in low circumstances was inducted to engage as a Substitute (the pay for which I was shamefully cheated of) and was mustered into service the tenth of Jany following and marched and at the battle of the horse Shoe on the Tallapoose was wounded first by a bullet in the fleshy part of the right arm which occasioned a considerable loss of blood the second wound a bullet in my left Groin which ranged back and Lodged and since my return home was cut out with a knife the third a bullet in the right breast which glanced coming out under my Arm my fourth was from the blow of a club which split my breast bone and laid me prostrate with the earth at the same moment an Indian mounted me to take a trophy from my head but was fortunately prevented a fellow soldier Bayoneting him in the attempt in this situation I lay on the battle ground until nearly dark when I was removed to my tent and when Doctor Acklen [Colonel Alsander J. Acklen] came he thought it not worth while to do anything for me for I was a dead man I sent for Doctor [Thomas] brown who attended about midnight and dressed my wounds and was removed to fort Williams where I slowly recovered and in June was able to move about my breast was and still continues to be my greatest misery particularly when aggravated by a cold when it seems to open and I am obliged to tie a handcherchief round me the wound in my Groin prevents me measurably from walking particularly on hilly ground and allways with pain and on the changes of Weather and when I go to rest am constly afflicted with pains and can only rest a while on my back and right side.

I have a wife and seven children to support by my industry the eldest beginning to help me

I did think I could struggle along without being a charge to my country but my strength and my constitution decrease and I respectfully ask of my country such pension as I may be thought to deserve and shall receive it with gratitude I am Sir your Hble servt Jesse Webb

Source: Jesse Webb, Veteran's Pension File, Invalid File 317, Records of the Veterans Administration, Record Group 15, National Archives and Records Administration, Washington, D.C.

XX. Sworn statement by Dempsey Parker, a private, Capt. Long's Company, 39th United States Infantry, July 18, 1848

State of Tennessee
Macon County

On this 18th day of July in the Year 1848 Personally appeared before the Circuit Court held for the County & State aforesaid in Open Court it being a of Court of Record Present the Hon. Andrew J. Marchbanks. Dempsey Parker a resident citizen of Macon County & State of Tennessee aged fifty six years, who being first duly sworn according to law doth on his oath make the following declaration. . . . That he enlisted in the Service of the United States in the County of Dixon State of Tennessee under Michael Clark Moulton recruiting Officer and was mustered into service at the Barracks four miles south of Nashville on the 26th day of December 1813 that he enlisted for the term of twelve months from that date and was attached to the Company Commanded by Capt. Alfred H. Douglass which company belonged to the thirty ninth Regiment of Infantry Commanded by Col. John Williams & Thomas H. Benton Lieutenant Colonel, that the Regiment to which he belonged was marched to Fort Deposit on the South Western bank of Tennessee River from thence to Fort Strowder [Strother] on the Coosa River to the place commonly called the Ten Islands, from thence to the mouth of Cedar Creek or Fort Williams, about which time Capt. Douglass was taken sick and left the Army and the Command of said Company devolved on Samuel Wilson who was first Lieutenant in the Company; until Capt. John B. Long took Command of said Company, from thence we were marched to the Horse Shoe bend on Tallapoosa River against the war party of the Creek nation of Indians, that while in the service of the United States engaged with the hostile Indians in the battle of the Horse Shoe bend in that action he received a wound in the joint of the left shoulder from a Spike fixed on the end of an arrow which was directed and shot by the enemy while near their breast works engaged in a personal encounter with one of the Savages which caused the gun of declarant to fall from his hands and he made several ineffectual attempts to draw the said Spike and was at length forced to twist the same before being enabled to extract it from his shoulder and drew a portion of flesh with it and was then Ordered by a non-Commissioned Officer to the Hospital prepared for the wounded and remained in the Hospital then, & at Fort Williams for near two months during which time he was not able to perform duty, that for the balance of his term of Service he was partially disabled, being incapable of performing any laborious duty, that the action of the Horse Shoe bend took place on Sunday the 27th day of March AD 1814.

From Fort Williams he was marched to the Hickory Grounds at Fort Jackson From thence to old Fort Stoddard or Mt. Vernon on or near the Mobile River, thence to Holmes's old field where Fort Montgomery was built, where he remained until he was discharged and received his Certificate of discharge from Capt Thomas Stewart of the 39th Regiment of Infantry, said Stuart being the highest Officer in Command at Fort Montgomery at the time he received his said Certificate of discharge which is here filed as part of this Declaration marked No. 1 After receiving which he returned home to Dixon County Tennessee where he resided until the following Spring. at which time the wound in his shoulder became inflamed and *suppuration* in several places ensued and for which he was under medical treatment for a considerable length of time. his shoulder gradually perishing away and leaving him in a great degree disabled in the use of the left arm and shoulder resulting from said wound and several times since the shoulder has become inflamed from said wound and for the last two years he has been a greater portion of the time totally disabled in said shoulder and arm. . . .

Dempsey Parker

Source: Dempsey Parker, Veteran's Pension File, Invalid File 16596, Records of the Veterans Administration, Record Group 15, National Archives and Records Administration, Washington, D.C.

XXI. Statement by Andrew Jackson from the Pension Application of George Mayfield[20]

Be it remembered that George Mayfield who is now an applicant for a pension as the within papers shew, was a private in Captain John Gordons Company of Spies during the Creek war of 1813 & 14—and acted as my Interpreter.—At the Battle of the Horseshoe or Tehopoka Mr. Mayfield was ordered to accompany me near one angle of the Indian Breastwork (where they had covered themselves with brushwood and was firing upon & killing our men—from our position it was impossible for the Indians to escape—but when we had advanced within thirty paces of their Breastworks I directed Mr. Mayfield (under cover of a Black Oak[)] to speak to them in their own Language. He hailed them—and they ceased firing—when he was directed to say to them, they could not escape, but if they would surrender they should be preserved & humanely treated, they replied by a discharge of their guns—and from our exposed situation, their aim being at my head as I supposed—the Ball struck the hard bark of the Black oak glanced by my head & penetrated the Right shoulder of Mr. Mayfield—giving him a severe wound—which deprived him of the use of it for a great while.—The valuable services of Mr. Mayfield during the Creek War with this severe wound, entitles him to a Pension as much as any soldier wounded under my command.

Andrew Jackson

Source: George Mayfield, Veteran's Pension File, Invalid File 194, Records of the Veterans Administration, Record Group 15, National Archives and Records Administration, Washington, D.C.

XXII. Sworn statement by Black Prince [Cahlahsayohha], a Cherokee veteran, served as 3rd Corporal in Capt. John Speers's [Arnekayan] Company

Cherokee Nation, Illinois District: Personally appeared before me the Subscriber Black Prince a free man of Colour who being duly sworn says, that he did actually serve in the Regiment of Cherokee Indians commanded by Col Gideon Morgan who was engaged on the side of the United States during the late war with Great Britain, that he was under the command of Captain John Spears, & while in the said service and engaged in Battle at the Horse Shoe on the 27th March 1814 he was wounded by a gun shot, the ball entering & passing through the right thigh just above the knee, that in consequence of said wound, he was seriously disabled, that he now resides in Delaware District, Cherokee Nation & that Capt John Spears under whom he served is now dead. Black Prince his X mark

> Sworn to and Subscribed before me this 27th of March AD 1848 Nicholas B. McNair

Source: Black Prince, Veteran's Pension File, File No. 21, 147, Records of the Veterans Administration, Record Group 15, National Archives and Records Administration, Washington, D.C.[21]

Accounts Detailing the Red Stick Experience

XXIII. Excerpt from Thomas McKenney's published account of Menawa, the Okfuskee war chief who survived the battle, compiled from accounts of Creek survivors[22]

We pass over a number of engagements that occurred in this war, in several of which Menawa acted a leading part . . . passing on to the great battle of the Horseshoe, wherein it was the fate of this chief to act and suffer as became the military head of a gallant people. . . .

The comrades of Menawa followed him into the battle, and fought at his side with desperate valour, until nearly all were slain, and he fell wounded by seven balls. . . .

When the storm of the battle subsided, Menawa remained on the field, lying in a heap of the slain, devoid of consciousness. Recovering his senses, he found himself weltering in blood, with his gun firmly grasped in his hand. The battle had ceased, or swept by, but straggling shots announced that the work of death was not over. Raising himself slowly to a sitting posture, he perceived a soldier passing near him, whom, with a deliberate aim, he shot, but at the same moment received a severe wound from a bullet, which, entering his check near the ear, and carrying away several of his teeth, passed out on the opposite side of the face. Again he fell among the dead, retaining, however, so much of life as to feel the victors treading upon his body as they passed over it, supposing him to be slain. When night came he felt revived, and the love of life grew strong in him. He crawled cautiously to the bank of the river, and descending to its margin found a canoe, which he entered, and by shaking it from side to side loosed it from the shore. The canoe floated down the river until it reached the neighbourhood of the swamp at Elkahatchee, where the Indian women and children had been secreted previous to the battle. Some of these wretched beings, who were anxiously looking out for intelligence from the scene of action, espied the canoe, and upon going to it, discovered the mangled chief laying nearly insensible it its bottom.

Menawa was removed to a place of rendezvous which had been appointed on the Elkahatchee creek, where he was joined by the unhappy survivors of that dreadful battle. For the purpose of brooding over their grief, mourning for the dead, and deciding upon the measures necessary to be adopted in consequence of the recent disaster, a silent council was held, that lasted three days, during which time these moody warriors neither ate, nor drank, nor permitted their wounds to be dressed. As the expiration of the third day it was determined that the Indians should return to their respective homes, submit to the victors, and each man make his own peace as best he might. Their wounds were then dressed by the women, who usually officiate as surgeons. . . .

They soon dispersed, and all of them surrendered formally to the American authorities, except Menawa, whose wounds prevented him from leaving his retreat until after the close of the war. As soon as he was able to travel he sought his home, at the Oakfuskee towns, but found neither shelter nor property. The desolating hand of war had swept all away. . . .

Source: Thomas McKenney, *History of the Indian Tribes of North America, with Biographical Sketches and Anecdotes of the Principal Chiefs*, vol. 2 (Philadelphia: Frederick W. Greenough, 1838), 97–105.

XXIV: An account of Johnie Benson (Tul-wa Tus-tun-ug-gee) during the Creek War, excerpted from the diary of his descendant, Chief George Washington Grayson[23]

Of his earlier youth we have no information; but know that sometime during his early manhood he was prevailed upon by the powerful oratory of the Indian promoters of war to join the ranks of the hostile Creeks, sometimes designated as the "Red Sticks," who arose up in arms against the United States government. And true to his martial name of *warrior*, [he] fought to very desperation under the leadership of Mun-ah-we against the United States forces under general Andrew Jackson. Notably at the battle of the *Horse Shoe Bend* where the Red Sticks had made a determined stand, he was wounded nine . . . times, which in later life proved the source of ever-recurring pain and illness, some attacks lasting many days in duration. These attacks were caused, as it was said, by the fact that the bullets were never extruded by the Indian doctors who treated his wounds.

In the foregoing mentioned engagement [Tul-wa Tus-tun-ug-gee] was completedly disabled by his many wounds. When the day was spent and darkness came on and the Creeks recognizing the fact that they could not continue the contest longer were retiring under the cover of night, but for his brother E-mah-thla-hut-ky and other comrades, he would have been left upon the field to the mercy of the enemy who would come upon the grounds the next morning. This brother with the assistance of others took him upon his back, and in company with their retiring comrades, he was born to a place of safety in the woods miles away where the Indian medicine men doctored him and after many weeks, restored him to fairly good health.

Source: Excerpted from W. David Baird, ed., *A Creek Warrior for the Confederacy: The Autobiography of Chief G. W. Grayson* (Norman: University of Oklahoma Press, 1988), 23–24.

XXV. Excerpt of a letter from Benjamin Hawkins to Secretary of War John Armstrong, June 21, 1814

The "Red Clubs" are making their peace as fast as they can, and receiving food from us. Our stock as yet affords but a scanty supply. I have a family here who were wealthy, and lost all their property by their delusion. One of the men was at the Horseshoe fort, taken by General [Andrew] Jackson, wounded in two or three places, and escaped by remaining in the water with his nose only out, till night, and made his way in the dark. He represents the fate of his party from the combined attack of their opponents like the fall of leaves.

Source: Published in Walter Lowrie and Walter S. Franklin, eds., *American State Papers: Documents, Legislative and Executive, of the Congress of the United States, Class II: Indian Affairs* (Washington, D.C., 1832), 1:859.

Appendix A *Known Manuscript Maps Depicting the Battle of Horseshoe Bend*

1. Cheatham Map. Map by Col. John A. Cheatham, Jackson's topographical engineer. National Archives, RG77, CWMF-Misc. 11–2. Map of Horseshoe Bend Battlefield, 1814.
2. Cheatham Map #2. Enclosed in William Bradford to General William Henry Harrison, April 5, 1814. William Henry Harrison Papers, Library of Congress, Manuscript Division. Unsigned but near identical copy of official Cheatham map (#1 above), also referred to as the Bradford map.
3. Ervin Map. Hugh Ervin's map of the Battle of Horseshoe Bend, 1814. Mississippi Department of Archives and History.
4. Cheatham Map #3. Untitled map with no attribution. Catalog title: Plan of Bend and Breast Works of Tohopeka, the Battle of the 27th March 1814. Untitled pen-and-ink manuscript map dated 1814. 42 x 33 cm. Library of Congress, Geography and Map Division. [A derivative copy of the Cheatham map and likely the basis for the engraved map that appeared in John Eaton's *Life of Andrew Jackson* (1817). Eaton completed the book, which Reid had begun. This version does not show troop deployment or details of the battle. Perhaps copied by John Reid.]
5. Andrew Jackson's Map of the Horseshoe Bend Battleground. "Battle of Tehopiska." Bound with Jackson's report to Governor Blount of Tennessee, dated March 31, 1814. Believed to have been sketched by Jackson. Tennessee Historical Society Collections, Tennessee State Library and Archives.
6. Tarrant Map. "Map of the Battle of Horseshoe Bend, Battle Fought 27th March 1814, For Capt. Leonard L. Tarrant" (variously known as the Holmes or Coffee map).
7. Carroll Map. "Battle of the Horshoe fought 27 March 1814 as scetched by Col. Carroll (now Genl. Carroll) a few days after the battle to J. Graham." Joseph Graham Papers, State Archives of North Carolina.
8. McEwen, Robert Houston. "Sketch Map of the Battle of Horseshoe Bend of Tallapoosa River, 27th March 1814." Library of Congress, Geography & Map Division.
9. Tahopta. "Battle of Tahopta Fought the 27th of March 1814." Copy of manuscript map of unknown provenance. Tennessee State Library and Archives, Photograph Collection, Ac. No. 72–57. (Location of original unknown.)
10. Stephens Map. Isaac Stephens Map. Included in letter to Henry Mackey, May 12, 1814. Gilder Lehrman Institute of American History, GLC06772.
11. Tehoo[pca]. "Battle of Tehoo[pca]." 1814. Pen-and-ink, pencil, and watercolor. 21 x 13 cm. Library of Congress, Geography and Map Division.
12. Hand-drawn map of Horseshoe Bend dated 1814 May 15th. Sent to Rhea County, Tennessee. University of Tennessee Libraries, Knoxville, Betsey B. Creekmore Special Collections and University Archives, Map regarding the Battle of Horseshoe Bend, MS.0352.

Appendix B *Selected Early Published Maps Depicting the Battle of Horseshoe Bend*

1. *A draft of the scene of the action, taken by an officer on the spot. Niles Weekly Register*, May 7, 1814.
2. *The Battle of the Horse Shoe, 27th March 1814*. By John Reid. Published in John Henry Eaton, *The Life of Andrew Jackson . . . Commenced by John Reid . . . Completed by John Henry Eaton*. Philadelphia: M. Carey and Son, 1817. [Map insert follows p. 176]
3. *To-Ho-Pe-Ka or The Horse-Shoe*. Colored engraving. Published in Charles E. Lester, *The Life of Sam Houston: The Hunter, Patriot, and Statesman of Texas*. Philadelphia: Davis, Porter & Coates, 1866.
4. *Battle of Tohopeka*. Black-and-white engraving. Published in Amos Kendall, *Life of Andrew Jackson*. New York: Harper & Brothers, 1843. Based on Cheatham's map. [Map insert follows p. 216]
5. *Battle of Cholocco Litabixee; or, The Horse-Shoe*. Black-and-white engraving. Published in Albert J. Pickett, *History of Alabama, and Incidentally of Georgia and Mississippi, from the Earliest Period*. 2 Vols. Charleston: Walker and James, 1851. Based on Cheatham's map.
6. *The Battle of the Horse Shoe*. Black-and-white engraving. Derived from *Pickett's History of Alabama*. Published in Benson John Lossing, *The Pictorial Field-Book of the War of 1812*. New York: Harper & Brothers, 1869.

Appendix C *Maps Mentioned in the Documentary Record but Not Located or Positively Identified*

1. "I send you a hasty sketch taken by the eye of the situation in which the enemy were encamped, & of the manner in which I approached them." Andrew Jackson to Thomas Pinckney, On the Battle ground on bend of the Tallapoosa 28th March 1814, Record Group 49, Letters Received by the Secretary of War, Registered Series, M221 roll 56.[1]
2. "I herewith send you a plat of the river and bend, where we fought for your satisfaction to see our movements." John Coffee to Mary Donelson Coffee, April 2, 1814. Dyas Collection, Coffee Papers, Accession # : 38, Box 3, Folder 13, Tennessee State Archives.
3. "I enclose you a plan of the bend of the River together with the fortifications and situations of both the Infantry & Cavalry." Lieutenant Alexander McCulloch to Frances McCulloch, McCulloch Papers, April 1, 1813 [1814], University of Texas.
4. "The draft which Lieutenant Rice encloses, will give you a better description of the place than I can, to which I refer you." Gideon Morgan to Governor Blount, April 1, 1814. Letter published on April 12, 1814, in the *Clarion and Tennessee State Gazette*.
5. *A Draft of the Scene of the Action, Taken by an Officer on the Spot*, rendered in print, *Pittsburg Mercury*, April 27, 1814.

Notes

Preface

1. For a thorough discussion of the rise of commercial manufactured maps, see Martin Brückner, *The Social Life of Maps in America, 1750–1860* (Chapel Hill, 2017), particularly chapter 2.

2. The original edition of the *Military Atlas* appeared in late 1813. The 1815 edition contained, in addition to the Creek War map, a map of New Orleans.

3. The Alabama Department of Archives and History owns the manuscript map of the Battle of Talladega. A printed version, "A Sketch of the Battle of Talladega," was published in John Reid and John Henry Eaton's *The Life of Andrew Jackson* (Philadelphia, 1817). The sketch of Fort Mims, found among the papers of General Ferdinand Leigh Claiborne, is also housed at the Alabama Department of Archives and History. They also hold a crude sketch of the famous "Canoe Fight" on the Alabama River.

Chapter 1. The Battle of Horseshoe Bend

1. For background on the early phases of the war and the Red Stick assault on Fort Mims, see Gregory A. Waselkov, *A Conquering Spirit: Fort Mims and the Redstick War of 1813–1814* (Tuscaloosa, Ala., 2006).

2. A number of excellent studies cover the Creek War, beginning with the still valuable work by Henry S. Halbert and Timothy H. Ball, *The Creek War of 1813–1814* (Montgomery, Ala., 1895). More recent studies include Claudio Saunt, *A New Order of Things: Property, Power, and the Transformation of the Creek Indians, 1733–1816* (Cambridge, Mass., 1999); Kevin Kokomoor, *Of One Mind and of One Government: The Rise and Fall of the Creek Nation in the Early Republic* (Lincoln, Nebr., 2018); and Tom Kanon, *Tennesseans at War, 1812–1815: Andrew Jackson, the Creek War, and the Battle of New Orleans* (Tuscaloosa, Ala., 2014).

3. For the Battle of Horseshoe Bend, see James W. Holland, *Andrew Jackson and the Creek War: Victory at the Horseshoe* (Tuscaloosa, Ala., 1990); and Tom Kanon, "'A Slow, Laborious Slaughter': The Battle of Horseshoe Bend," *Tennessee Historical Quarterly* 58 (Spring 1999): 3–15.

4. Andrew Jackson to Willie Blount, March 31, 1814 (document IV in this volume). Published in John Spenser Bassett, ed., *Correspondence of Andrew Jackson*, 7 vols. (Washington, D.C., 1926), 1:490. In a letter to James Baxter, Jackson stated the figure of "about one thousand" came from "our intelligent Cherokee Squaw who had been a prisoner with them." Andrew Jackson to James Baxter, April 1, 1814, Library of Congress (LOC), Jackson Papers, vol. 18, Doc. 1596.

5. "Extract of a Letter from a Distinguished Officer, Dated 6 Miles from New Youchaw, March 29th, 1814," *Clarion and Tennessee State Gazette*, April 12, 1814 (document II in this volume).

6. The officer was William Carroll and the quotation is taken from a note on his map, "Battle of the Horshoe fought 27 March 1814 as scetched by Colo. (now Genl. Carroll) a few days after the battle," Joseph Graham Papers, North Carolina State Archives, Raleigh. For an account of the battle and its importance, see *Tohopeka: Rethinking the Creek War & War of 1812*, ed. Kathryn E. Holland Braund (Tuscaloosa, Ala., 2012). The Americans counted 557 dead Red Sticks on the ground and estimated an additional 250–300 in the river. Total American losses were 55 killed and 146 wounded. At least 350 women and children were taken prisoner; fatalities for noncombatants were not reported. In comparison, scholars estimate between 50 and 100 Indigenous deaths at the Battle of Tippecanoe. John Sugden, *Tecumseh: A Life* (New York, 1997), 235–36; Donald Hickey, *Tecumseh's War: The*

Epic Conflict for the Heart of America, 1811–1815 (Yardley, Pa., 2023), 53.

7. Regarding the counting of enemy dead, Jackson merely noted the total "found by officers of great respectability whom I had ordered to count them." Andrew Jackson to Willie Blount, March 31, 1814, in Bassett, *Correspondence of Andrew Jackson*, 1:491 (document IV in this volume).

8. In his report to Blount, Jackson reported the sixteen "had concealed themselves under the banks." Andrew Jackson to Willie Blount, March 31, 1814, in Bassett, *Correspondence of Andrew Jackson*, 1:492 (document IV in this volume).

9. The decision to "sink" the American dead in the river was a precaution to prevent Red Sticks from scalping and stripping the dead of their clothing, as some of the dead Red Sticks at Horseshoe Bend were found wearing clothing from those Americans buried on-site at the Battle of Emuckfaw. John Reid and John Henry Eaton, *The Life of Andrew Jackson* (Philadelphia, 1817), 155.

10. McEwen was the regimental quartermaster of Colonel John Brown's East Tennessee volunteers. Sketch map of the Battle of Horseshoe Bend of Tallapoosa River, March 27, 1814, Library of Congress.

11. Map by Colonel John A. Cheatham, Jackson's topographical engineer. Enclosed in William Bradford to General William Henry Harrison, April 5, 1814, William Henry Harrison Papers, National Archives, RG77, CWMF-Misc. 11–2, Map of Horseshoe Bend Battlefield, 1814. This map was sent to General William Henry Harrison.

12. The only other Creek War battles memorialized by contemporary mapmakers were Fort Mims and Talladega. A sketch found in the papers of Ferdinand Claiborne at the Alabama Department of Archives shows the layout of buildings and fortification around the house of Samuel Mims and provides locational and site details, including the major road, ferry crossing, fields, and woodlands. John Reid's biography of Jackson contained a map of the Battle of Talladega, a manuscript of which is housed by the Alabama Department of Archives and History. This map, unlike the HOBE maps, displays the disposition of hostile forces. The provenance of this pencil-on-paper map is uncertain, and it appears to have been crafted as an illustration for Reid's work rather than a battlefield production. The cartographer is unknown. The Alabama Department of Archives and History also owns a pencil sketch, done years after the battle, of the famous canoe battle involving Jeremiah Austill. A crude sketch on the reverse of a document in the Andrew Jackson papers has been tentatively identified as Fort Strother. Maps of Forts Bainbridge, Decatur, and Jackson, presumably drawn by a member of Colonel Graham's staff, are contained in his papers.

13. Jackson's assistant topographical engineer, Leroy May, resigned on March 14, 1814, and Jackson immediately appointed Cheatham to replace him. Cheatham was Jackson's sole cartographer during the engagement. His principal topographical engineer, John Strother, had resigned on February 26. Compiled Muster Roll for East and West Tennessee Militia at the Battle of Horseshoe Bend, on file, Horseshoe Bend National Military Park, Daviston, Alabama. For Cheatham's appointment, see John Reid to John A. Cheatham, March 14, 1814, Andrew Jackson Papers, Series 1, General Correspondence and Related Items, Library of Congress. See also Harold D. Moser, David R. Hoth, Sharon Macpherson, and John H. Reinbold, eds., *The Papers of Andrew Jackson*, vol. 3: *1814–1815* (Knoxville, Tenn., 1991), 426.

14. John A. Cheatham, War of 1812 Pension File, National Archives. Cheatham attained the rank of colonel before he mustered out. His rank at the time of the battle is unclear. Index to Compiled Service Records of Volunteer Soldiers Who Served during the War of 1812, NARA, M602; War of 1812 Pension and Bounty Land Warrant Application Files, RG15, NARA.

15. RG77-CWMR-Miss 11–2, Map of Horseshoe Bend Battlefield, 1814, NARA.

16. Andrew Jackson to Thomas Pinckney, March 28, 1814, in Moser et al., *The Papers of Andrew Jackson*, 3:52–53. The original is found in Letters Received by the Secretary of War, Registered Series, 1801–1860, National Archives, M221, Roll 56 (document I in this volume). Major General Thomas Pinckney was Jackson's immediate commander following the federalization of Tennessee state troops. Moser et al., *The Papers of Andrew Jackson*, 3:4. Pinckney forwarded a copy of Jackson's letter, and presumably the map, to Secretary of War John Armstrong. The map dispatched by Jackson from the battlefield is generally identified as Cheatham's map (figure 7 in this volume: RG77-CWMR-Miss 11–2, Map of Horseshoe Bend Battlefield, 1814, NARA), but that identification is problematic since part of the map was drawn to scale. It seems more likely that the map dispatched by Jackson from the battlefield was Cheatham's preliminary sketch, which was revised later to show the scale of the "bend" and the enemy defense works. This preliminary "hasty sketch" has not been located. Jackson sent a number of maps to Pinckney during his campaign. For example, see Andrew Jackson to Thomas Pinckney, March 23, 1815, in which he describes the location where he has established Fort William, referencing a map he has previously provided. Moser et al., *The Papers of Andrew Jackson*, 3:51.

17. Report of Andrew Jackson [to General Thomas Pinckney], April 5, 1814. The letter was printed in the *Nashville Whig* on May 25, 1814 (document XVII in this volume). The copy of the original letter can be found in Letters Received by the Secretary of War, Unregistered Series, 1789–1860, M222, Roll 12, National Archives. Governor Blount is sometimes incorrectly identified as the recipient of the letter.

18. Map by Colonel John A. Cheatham, Jackson's topographical engineer, also known as the Bradford map. Enclosed in William Bradford to William Henry Harrison, April 5, 1814, William H. Harrison Papers, Reel 2: Series 1, 1813–September 1839, Library of Congress, Manuscript Division.

19. Bradford to Harrison, April 5, 1814, Harrison Papers, LOC (document XVI in this volume).

20. MA/98.0171(a). The map is 32 cm × 40 cm. Hugh Ervin is listed on the 1816 Mississippi Territorial Census for Marion County: one adult male and one female over twenty, sixteen slaves. *Mississippi, State and Territorial Census Collection, 1792–1866* [database online] (Provo, Utah: Ancestry.com, 2007); original data: Mississippi State and Territorial Censuses, 1792–1866, microfilm V229, 3 rolls, Heritage Quest.

21. Index to Compiled Military Service Records for the Volunteer Soldiers Who Served during the War of 1812, NARA. The map is held in the David W. Haley Family Papers. Haley served as a major in the army during the War of 1812 and later surveyed Choctaw cessions and was a state senator. Pension records indicate that a David W. Haley was a private in the Tennessee militia (Captain Morgan's company and Captain Henderson's company). Records do not reveal that either Ervin or Haley was at Horseshoe Bend.

22. *The Tennessean*, March 19, 1884.

23. "Battle of Tehopiska or the Horseshoe: Report of Gen. Andrew Jackson to Gov. Willie Blount," *American Historical Magazine* 4 (October 1899): 291–96. The letter is also published in Bassett, *Correspondence of Andrew Jackson*, 1:489–92. The original bound letter and document are owned by the Tennessee Historical Society, THS T-100. Following its publication in William Robertson Garrett and Albert Virgil Goodpasture's *History of Tennessee: Its People and Its Institutions, from the Earliest Times to the Year 1903* (Nashville, 1903), the map was widely copied and distributed.

24. Thomas Kanon, an archivist with the Tennessee State Archives, where the Tennessee Historical Society manuscript collection is housed, is also a leading scholar of the Creek War and notes "tradition has it that Jackson personally drew this map, but that has never been verified." *Tennesseans at War*, 118.

25. Map of the Battle of Horseshoe Bend, Alabama Department of Archives and History, A-44. The map is 33 cm × 30 cm.

26. *Index to the Compiled Military Service Records for the Volunteer Soldiers Who Served during the War of 1812* (Washington, D.C.: NARA), M602, roll 204; Byron Sistler and Samuel Sistler, comps., *Tennesseans in the War of 1812* (Nashville, 1992), 487. Benton would later become second-in-command of the U.S. Thirty-Ninth Regiment.

27. Compiled Muster Roll for East and West Tennessee Militia at the Battle of Horseshoe Bend, on file, Horseshoe Bend National Military Park, Daviston, Alabama; Tom Kanon, "Regimental Histories of Tennessee Units during the War of 1818," on file at the Tennessee State Library and Archives.

28. 1860 United States Federal Census.

29. ADAH catalog notes; Grant Foreman, *Indian Removal: The Emigration of the Five Civilized Tribes of Indians* (Norman, Okla., 1966), 116. In the fall of 1836, Tarrant was appointed by Thomas Jesup as certifying agent for land contracts under the Treaty of Washington (1832) by which each Creek head of household was allotted 640 acres. Thomas Jesup to Leonard Tarrant, August 9, 1836, Letters Received by the Office of the Adjutant General, Main Series, 1822–1860, RG94 (Washington, D.C.: NARA), M567, roll 145. As the land certifying agent, Tarrant had a reputation for fairness. As one early history opined, "He was faithful to his trust. The sharpers tried to deceive him, and to bribe him. He was hard to deceive and could not be bribed. When the land traders had tried him, and found him forever on the side of right, and always on the side of the poor savage against the swindler, thy offered him a large sum of money to vacate, or resign his office, but he could not be bought." He was "a terror to the swindler." Anson West, *A History of Methodism in Alabama* (Nashville, 1893), 473. The family Bible records that Carolyn Virginia was born October 9, 1813, in Winchester, Tennessee. She married James A. Hogan on October 10, 1834. "The Family of Judge Leonard Tarrant," Mary A. Taylor Collection, Armstrong-Osborne Public Library, Talladega, Alabama.

30. "Battle of the Horshoe fought 27 March 1814 as scetched by Colo. Carrol (now Genl. Carroll) a few days after the battle," Joseph Graham Papers, North Carolina State Archives, Raleigh, North Carolina. Carroll was inspector general of West Tennessee and was instrumental in recruiting for Jackson. On Jackson's promotion to major general in the U.S. Army on May 28, 1814, Carroll was promoted to major general of the Tennessee militia. This occurred in May 1814.

31. The handwriting does not appear to be Graham's. All the sketches of forts and the battlefield include similar symbolism: rows

of dots for personnel, identical symbols for cannon. Other sketches and diagrams depict Forts Bainbridge, Decatur, Burrows, and Jackson. The likely candidate for the artist is Graham's aide-de-camp, Henry William Connor (based on author's analysis of handwriting). Connor later served as a representative from North Carolina. He died in 1866. William Henry Connor Pension File, Record Group 15: Records of the Department of Veterans Affairs, 1773–2007, War of 1812 Pension and Bounty Land Warrant Application Files, NARA. Carroll's original has not been located.

32. McEwen's papers are held by the Tennessee Historical Society and housed at the Tennessee State Library and Archives. His map resides in the Library of Congress. His mother was Sam Houston's aunt. His wife, Hetty Montgomery Kennedy, was the sister of William Kennedy.

33. The copy was donated to the Tennessee State Library and Archives by Lee Burnett of Toledo, Ohio. The copy resides in the Tennessee State Library and Archives Photograph Collection, ac. no. 73–57.

34. Isaac Stephens to Henry Mackey, account of Battle of Horseshoe Bend, with drawing, Gilder Lehrman Collection, #GLC06772. Stephens was born in Botetourt County, Virginia, in 1782, and died in Bledsoe County, Tennessee, in 1862. Find a Grave, https://www.findagrave.com/memorial/94866639/isaac-stephens.

35. Carroll Van West, *Tennessee's Historic Landscapes: A Traveler's Guide* (Knoxville, 1995), 270–71.

36. Battle of Tehoo[pca], G3972 .H6S42 1814.B3, Vault, Map Division, Library of Congress. The catalog card erroneously notes the battle involved "Andrew Jackson vs. Indian Chief Wetherhead [*sic*]." The map was obtained from Paul H. North Jr. in July 1953 but contains no other information about the cartographer or accompanying material.

37. Map Regarding the Battle of Horseshoe Bend, MS.0352, University of Tennessee Libraries, Knoxville, Betsey B. Creekmore Special Collections and University Archives, University of Tennessee, Knoxville, Tennessee (originally cataloged as Rhea County 15th May 1814). The reverse is littered with doodling and what appears to be penmanship practice. The top corner contains the faint name, J. R. Taylor, presumably the intended recipient.

38. McEwen map.

39. Map of the Battle of Horseshoe Bend, Battle Fought 27th March 1814, for Capt. Leonard L. Tarrants, Alabama Department of Archives and History. This map is variously known as the Holmes map since J. L. Holmes drew it or the Coffee map, presumably because Coffee's name is prominently shown but perhaps because Coffee was known to have produced a map, which is yet unidentified.

40. Andrew Jackson to Thomas Pinckney, April 5, 1814, *Nashville Whig*, May 25, 1814 (document XVII in this volume).

41. Andrew Jackson to Willie Blount, March 31, 1814, Bassett, *Correspondence of Andrew Jackson*, 1:490 (document IV in this volume).

Chapter 2. The Barricade

1. From descriptive text that accompanies "Battle of the Horshoe fought 27 March 1814 as scetched by Colo. Carroll (now Genl. Carroll) a few days after the battle." Joseph Graham Papers, North Carolina State Archives, Raleigh.

2. Bradford to Harrison, April 5, 1814, William H. Harrison Papers, LOC (document XVI in this volume).

3. Col. William Carroll to an Unnamed Friend, April 1, 1814, *Clarion and Tennessee State Gazette*, April 12, 1814 (document V in this volume). The bombardment began at 10:30 a.m. Jackson to Blount, March 31, 1814, in John Spenser Bassett, ed., *Correspondence of Andrew Jackson*, 7 vols. (Washington, D.C., 1926), 1:489–92 (document IV in this volume). The frontal attack on the barricade commenced at 12:30 p.m. Jackson to Perkins, April 1, 1814, *Nashville Whig*, April 27, 1814 (document XI in this volume). Grapeshot is specifically designed as an antipersonnel weapon and is ineffective as a battering weapon, as Jackson knew.

4. The Whale's Cherokee name is rendered in a variety of ways including Tucfo, Tuck Wah, and Tuq-qua. He and his son-in-law, Second Corporal Charles Reese, and another unnamed Cherokee were the initial swimmers. For more on Cherokee participation in the Creek War, see Susan M. Abram, *Forging a Cherokee-American Alliance in the Creek War: From Creation to Betrayal* (Tuscaloosa, Ala., 2015). For information on the presentation rifle awarded to The Whale by the United States for his actions during the battle, see Brad Agnew, "The Whale's Rifle," *Chronicles of Oklahoma* 4(Winter 1978–1979): 472–77; Peter Brannon, "Whale's Rifle," *Arrow Points* 6 (January 1923): 47–49; and Justin Weiss, "The Whale Rifle," PDF of online exhibit, on file at Horseshoe Bend National Military Park.

5. John Coffee to John Donelson, April 1, 1814, Coffee Papers, Tennessee State Library and Archives. Coffee could not have observed this firsthand from his rear position, but it is mentioned by others (document VI in this volume).

6. Andrew Jackson to Willie Blount, March 31, 1814, Tennessee Historical Society/Tennessee State Archives; Quotation from John Reid to his father, April 5, 1814, John Reid Papers, 1802–1842, Library of Congress (documents IV and XVIII in this volume).

7. John Reid to his father, April 5, 1814, John Reid Papers, 1802–1842, Library of Congress (document XVIII in this volume).

8. Stephen Routh, Granger County, Tennessee, Pension application dated March 22, 1871, copy on file at Horseshoe Bend National Military Park.

9. Gideon Morgan to William G. Blount, April 1, 1814, *Clarion and Tennessee State Gazette*, April 12, 1814 (document XIII in this volume).

10. Charles C. Lester, *The Life of Sam Houston: The Hunter, Patriot, and Statesman of Texas* (Philadelphia, 1866), 33.

11. Andrew Jackson to Rachel Jackson, April 1, 1814, in Harold D. Moser, David R. Hoth, Sharon Macpherson, and John H. Reinbold, eds., *The Papers of Andrew Jackson*, vol. 3: *1814–1815* (Knoxville, Tenn., 1991), 54 (document X in this volume).

12. Moser et al., *The Papers of Andrew Jackson*, 3:65. The Americans left the battleground on the twenty-eighth, after making litters for the wounded and interring their own dead. Andrew Jackson to Thomas Pinckney, March 28,1814. Thus, there was no time (or desire) to bury enemy troops. In addition to lack of rations and the need to evacuate their own wounded, there was concern that a retaliatory strike might occur.

13. *Memorial of the Horseshoe Bend Battle Commission*, Senate Document No. 756, 60th Congress, 2d Session, March 3, 1909, 9.

14. For a history of the park, see Keith S. Hébert and Kathryn H. Braund, *Horseshoe Bend National Military Park Administrative History* (Washington, D.C., 2019).

15. Charles H. Fairbanks, "Report of Excavations at Horseshoe Bend National Military Park," February 1962, p. 3, on file, Horseshoe Bend National Military Park. See also "Excavations at Horseshoe Bend, Alabama," *Florida Anthropologist* 25 (June 1962): 41-55 and George C. Mackenzie, *The Indian Breastwork in the Battle of Horseshoe Bend: Its Size, Location, and Construction*, Report for the U.S. Department of the Interior, Division of History, Office of Archeology and Historic Preservation, November 24, 1969.

16. Quoted in Mackenzie, *Indian Breastwork*, 32.

17. Mackenzie, *Indian Breastwork*, 26–27. For information on the terracing program, see F. N. Farrington, "Tallapoosa County's Terracing Program," *Agricultural Engineering* 16 (1935): 313–16. The terracing operations that took place within the area eventually encompassed by the park is known as Cotton Patch Hill, deemed far from the Creek barricade, although the site of one of Fairbanks's trenches.

18. Mackenzie, *Indian Breastwork*, 32.

19. Mackenzie, *Indian Breastwork*, 50.

20. Mackenzie, *Indian Breastwork*, 49 (first quotation), 51 (second quotation), 50 (third quotation), 36 (fourth quotation), 37 (fifth quotation).

21. Mackenzie, *Indian Breastwork*, 43.

22. Mackenzie, *Indian Breastwork*, 36, appendix D.

23. Mackenzie, *Indian Breastwork*, 46–47 (quotations). See 47a–47b for conjectural diagrams.

24. James Parton, *The Life of Andrew Jackson*, 3 vols. (New York, 1861), 1:516.

25. Andrew Jackson to Rachel Jackson, April 1, 1814, in Moser et al., *The Papers of Andrew Jackson*, 3:54 (document X in this volume).

26. John to Betsy Reid, April 1, 1814, John Reid Papers, 1802–1842, Library of Congress (document XIV in this volume).

27. In addition to a report to the NPS, Dickens published his findings. Roy S. Dickens Jr., *Archaeological Investigations at Horseshoe Bend National Military Park, Alabama*, Special Publications of the Alabama Archaeological Society, No. 3, December 1979 (Tuscaloosa, Ala., 1979). Quotations from p. 195. He also conducted substantial investigations at the village and the Creek town of Nuyaka, and at the end of the season, an underwater archaeological survey was undertaken to find evidence of "caves" supposedly used by survivors fleeing the battle. For analysis and criticism of Dickens's barricade reconstruction, see Gregory A. Waselkov, "A Reinterpretation of the Creek Indian Barricade at Horseshoe Bend," *Journal of Alabama Archaeology* 32 (December 1986): 94–107. For further assessment of the proposed barricade reconstructions by Dickens and Waselkov, see Elizabeth de Grummond and Christine Hamlin, *Horseshoe Bend National Military Park: Archeological Overview and Assessment* (Tallahassee, Fla., 2000), 64–66. The Southeast Archeological Center (SEAC) was established as the NPS's archaeological support operation in the early 1990s. SEAC also provides curation and storage of artifacts from the Southeast region.

28. Waselkov, "A Reinterpretation of the Creek Indian Barricade at Horseshoe Bend," 98.

29. John E. Cornelison Jr., "A Metal Detecting Survey of the Palisade Area at Horseshoe Bend National Military Park," SEAC accession number 1838, Southeast Archeological Center, Tallahassee, Fla., 2006, 2.

30. For a discussion of the process, see Cornelison, "Metal Detecting Survey," 38–47. Jackson reported that he placed his artillery on

a hill that was "about eighty yards, & from its farthest, about two hundred and fifty" from the barricade. Andrew Jackson to Willie Blount, March 31, 1814, Tennessee Historical Society/Tennessee State Archives (document IV in this volume).

31. John E. Cornelison et al., "Barricade: Archeological and Geophysical Investigations at the Battle of Horseshoe Bend National Military Park," SEAC accession number 2611, i.

32. Cornelison, "Barricade," 71–74, quotation from p. 71.

33. Cornelison, "Barricade," quotations from pp. 11 and 68.

34. The sally port is noted as figure 2 on McEwen's map.

35. John Reid to "Dear Father," April 5, 1814, John Reid Papers, Library of Congress (document XVIII in this volume).

36. Lester, *Life of Sam Houston*, 34.

37. George Mayfield Pension Record, #149, Record Group 15, Records of the Veterans Administration, Veteran's Administration, Veteran's Pension Files (document XXI in this volume). See also Kathryn H. Braund, "'Resolved Not to Yield': Tohopeka Two Hundred Years On," *Alabama Review* 67 (July 2014): 213.

38. Gideon Morgan to William G. Blount, April 1, 1814, *Clarion and Tennessee State Gazette*, April 12, 1814 (document XIII in this volume).

39. For example, see John Coffee to John Donelson, April 1, 1814, Tennessee Historical Society Miscellaneous Files, Box 3, C-118, Tennessee State Library and Archives.

40. Jackson reported the capture of one young Red Stick on the 28th, who reported that nineteen others sheltering with him had escaped during the night. Andrew Jackson to Rachel Jackson, April 1, 1814, in Moser et al., *The Papers of Andrew Jackson*, 3:54–55 (document X in this volume). One frequently cited account was first relayed by H. S. Halbert in the 1880s. Halbert, who wrote a history of the Creek War, gathered information from Archibald Macarthy, an eighty-year-old Mississippi man who claimed he had heard stories from veterans of the battle when he was young. Macarthy related that soldiers had used "long wooden wedges" to split off a segment of a "shelving bluff of the river" and bury some Red Sticks alive. Some writers have linked this story to the deaths of the sixteen Red Sticks killed the day after the battle. See Tom Kanon, "'A Slow, Laborious Slaughter': The Battle of Horseshoe Bend," *Tennessee Historical Quarterly* 58 (Spring 1999): 15–28.

41. John Coffee to Andrew Jackson, April 1, 1814, Andrew Jackson Collection, 1788–1942, Tennessee State Library and Archives (document VII in this volume); and John Coffee to John Donelson, Tennessee Historical Society Miscellaneous Files, Box 3, C-118, Tennessee State Library and Archives (document VI in this volume).

42. Mackenzie, *Indian Breastwork*, 34–35.

43. Mackenzie, *Indian Breastwork*, 35.

44. Dickens, *Archaeological Investigations*, 195. In lieu of excavation at the cliff, his team conducted underwater archaeology in hopes of recovering artifacts but was unsuccessful in that effort. See Walter N. Doetzem, "Underwater Archaeology Project," published as appendix II in Dickens, *Archaeological Investigations*, 230–34.

45. For a succinct account of the army's action, see Jackson's official report to Thomas Pinckney, March 28, 1814, in Moser et al., *The Papers of Andrew Jackson*, 3:52–53 (document I in this volume). For "works," see John Coffee to Andrew Jackson, April 1, 1828, in Moser et al., *The Papers of Andrew Jackson*, 56 (document VII in this volume). In his letter to Rachel Jackson, the general noted that after his men "carried the works, by storm . . . [the] Indians took posesesion of the river bank, and part of their works raised with brush getting into the interior of the bend." Andrew Jackson to Rachel Jackson, April 1, 1814, in Moser et al., *The Papers of Andrew Jackson*, 3:54 (document X in this volume).

Chapter 3. Battle Maps as a Key to Understanding the Creek Response to the American Invasion

1. J. B. Harley, *The New Nature of Maps: Essays in the History of Cartography*, ed. Paul Laxton (Baltimore, 2002), 35–36.

2. Jerry Brotton, *A History of the World in Twelve Maps* (New York, 2012), 438.

3. Hand-drawn map detailing Battle of Horseshoe Bend, 1814 May 15th, Rhea County, Tennessee, Special Collections Library, University of Tennessee, Knoxville, Tenn.

4. "Battle of Tehopiska," Tennessee Historical Society Collections, the Tennessee State Library and Archives, T-100 Misc. Collection. The map was first published as "Battle of Tehopiska or the Horseshoe: Report of Gen. Andrew Jackson to Gov. Willie Blount," *American Historical Magazine* 4 (October 1899): 291–96.

5. William Carroll, letter of April 1, 1814, *Clarion and Tennessee State Gazette*, April 12, 1814 (document V in this volume).

6. Andrew Jackson to James Baxter, April 1, 1814, LOC, Jackson Papers, vol. 18, Doc. 1596.

7. John E. Cornelison Jr., "A Metal Detecting Survey of the Palisade Area at Horseshoe Bend National Military Park," SEAC Accession Number 1838, Southeast Archeological Center, Tallahassee, Fla., 2006, 9–10.

8. Lieutenant Bean was ordered to the island by John Coffee, who noted that action "had a very happy effect, as many of the enemy did attempt their escape to the Island, but not one ever landed, they were sunk by Leut. Beans command ere they reached the bank, and that few was killed the instant they landed." John Coffee to Andrew Jackson, April 1, 1814, in Harold D. Moser, David R. Hoth, Sharon Macpherson, and John H. Reinbold, eds., *The Papers of Andrew Jackson*, vol. 3: *1814–1815* (Knoxville, Tenn., 1991), 56 (document VII in this volume). The maps do not provide a name for the island. Isaac Stephens noted on his map, "An Island fixed for cultivation."

9. Alexander McCulloch to Frances McCulloch, April 1, 1813 [*sic*], Ben and Henry Eustace McCulloch Family Papers, Dolph Briscoe Center for American History, University of Texas at Austin (document XII in this volume). See Thomas W. Cutrer, ed., "'The Tallapoosa Might Truly Be Called the River of Blood': Major Alexander McCulloch and the Battle of Horseshoe Bend, March 27, 1813," *Alabama Review* 43 (January 1990): 35–39.

10. Cheatham's captions indicate that the town and habitations were "new." The representations of the structures vary in number and kind but do suggest log cabin construction of the kind beginning to become more prominent among the Creeks. Such cabins have been located archaeologically at Holy Ground. See Gregory A. Waselkov and Craig Sheldon, "Redstick Creek Log Cabins at the Holy Ground," in *Native American Log Cabins in the Southeast*, ed. Gregory A. Waselkov (Knoxville, Tenn., 2019), 45–66. For reference to the barricade as a "fort," see Waddy Tate to Caleb Tate, April 9, 1814, Library of Virginia, http://www.virginiamemory.com/blogs/out_of_the_box/2012/04/18/dear-uncle/#.T464abwK8MQ.facebook.

11. George Stiggins, "A Historical Narration of the Genealogy Traditions and Downfall of the Ispocaga or Creek Tribe of Indians, Written by One of the Tribe," Lyman Draper Collection, State Historical Society of Wisconsin.

12. Stiggins's account as well as that of Pickett have elevated Weatherford's leap to prominence in Alabama history. See Albert J. Pickett, *History of Alabama, and Incidentally of Georgia and Mississippi*, 2 vols. (Charleston, S.C., 1851), 2:322–25. The site has now been definitively located. See Gregory A. Waselkov, "Return to Holy Ground: The Legendary Battle Site Discovered," *Alabama Heritage*, no. 101 (Summer 2011): 28–37.

13. Andrew Jackson to Thomas Pinckney, January 29, 1814, in John Spenser Bassett, ed., *Correspondence of Andrew Jackson*, 7 vols. (Washington, D.C., 1926), 1:447.

14. Thomas L. McKenney and James Hall, *History of the Indian Tribes of North America with Biographical Sketches and Anecdotes of the Principal Chiefs* (Philadelphia, 1838), 100–101.

15. Andrew Jackson to Rachel Jackson, April 1, 1814, in Moser et al., *The Papers of Andrew Jackson*, 3:55 (document X in this volume).

16. Braund, "Reflections on 'Shee Coocys' and the Motherless Child: Creek Women in a Time of War," *Alabama Review* 64 (October 2011): 281–82. Americans also enslaved captive children, but there are no records of this occurring at Horseshoe Bend. Only a handful of Red Stick soldiers managed to escape the battlefield and all were severely wounded.

17. Frank L. Owsley Jr., *Struggle for the Gulf Borderlands: The Creek War and the Battle of New Orleans, 1812–1815* (Tuscaloosa, Ala., 2000), 82.

Chapter 4. Memorializing Sacrifice

1. Bradford to Harrison, April 5, 1814, William Henry Harrison Papers, LOC (document XVI in this volume).

2. Coffee to John Donelson, April 1, 1814, Tennessee Historical Society Miscellaneous Files, Box 3, C-118, Tennessee State Library and Archives (document VI in this volume).

3. The corpses of the slain Red Sticks were left on the battleground and the margins of the river.

4. Report of March 27, 1814, Record Group 107, Records of the Secretary of War, Letters Received, Unregistered Series, M222–12. The report was also printed in the *Nashville Clarion*, May 10, 1814. A copy, "Report of the Killed and Wounded in the Battle of Tohopeka," also resides in the Andrew Jackson Papers, Chicago Historical Society.

5. Jackson had earlier reported 26 killed and 105 wounded. Report of Andrew Jackson [to General Thomas Pinckney], April 5, 1814, *Nashville Whig*, May 25, 1814 (document XVII in this volume). Quantification of military strength was well established in the American military through the use of muster rolls, which tracked effective numbers of troops. In the same way, the army carefully noted its sick, wounded, and dead to assess strength and readiness and for purposes of payrolls.

6. Jackson to Pinckney, March 28, 1814, in Harold D. Moser, David R. Hoth, Sharon Macpherson, and John H. Reinbold, eds., *The Papers of Andrew Jackson*, vol. 3: *1814–1815* (Knoxville, Tenn., 1991), 52 (document I in this volume).

7. James Parton, *The Life of Andrew Jackson*, 3 vols. (New York, 1861), 1:518. Many, particularly Jackson's political opponents, were horrified

by the bloodletting, and it was a factor in his presidential campaign, particularly the death of sixteen the day after the battle.

8. Jackson to Blount, March 31, 1814, in John Spenser Bassett, ed., *Correspondence of Andrew Jackson*, 7 vols. (Washington, D.C., 1926), 1:491 (document IV in this volume).

9. "A Correct View of the Battle of the Hourse-Shoe, March 27th 1814." Map drawn by Isaac Stephens. Courtesy of the Gilder Lehrman Institute of American History.

10. "Battle of Tehopiska," Tennessee Historical Society Collections, Tennessee State Library and Archives, T-100, Misc. Collection. Montgomery's name is spelled correctly in Jackson's letter to Blount. A map published on May 7, 1814, in *Niles' Weekly Register* indicated the locations where Lieutenants Moulton and Somerville fell. The maps originally appeared in the *Pittsburg Mercury* with an explanation that the "draft of the scene of action" was drawn by "an officer on the spot" and promised they had attempted to faithfully render the map "with as much accuracy as the nature of letter-press printing will admit." The original map has not been located.

11. Andrew Jackson to Willie Blount, March 31, 1814, in Bassett, *Correspondence of Andrew Jackson*, 1:492 (document IV in this volume). The other men were Lieutenant Robert M. Somerville and Lieutenant Michael C. Moulton. See Andrew Jackson to Governor Blount, March 31, 1814, in Bassett, *Correspondence of Andrew Jackson*, 1:492. Jackson also described Montgomery's actions as "gallant" in a letter to Thomas Pinckney the day after the battle while characterizing that of Colonel John Williams as "skillful & intrepid." Andrew Jackson to Thomas Pinckney, Marcy 28, 1814, in Moser et al., *The Papers of Andrew Jackson*, 3:52 (document I in this volume). In reporting Montgomery's death to his wife, Jackson mentioned only Montgomery, who "bravely fell on the walls," omitting the names of the lieutenants. Andrew Jackson to Rachel Jackson, April 1, 1814, in Bassett, *Correspondence of Andrew Jackson*, 1:493, and Moser et al., *The Papers of Andrew Jackson*, 3:55 (document X in this volume).

12. Moulton is the seat of Lawrence County, and Somerville served as the first seat of Morgan County.

13. Copy of a letter from Major Reed [Reid] to a friend, March 28, 1814, *Clarion and Tennessee State Gazette*, April 12, 1814 (document III in this volume). Tom Kanon correctly notes that "Montgomery's death is mentioned in practically every account of the battle, official or otherwise." Tom Kanon, *Tennesseans at War, 1812–1815: Andrew Jackson, the Creek War, and the Battle of New Orleans* (Tuscaloosa, Ala., 2014), 102.

14. John Coffee to John Donelson, April 1, 1814, Coffee Papers, Box 25, file 2, the Tennessee State Library and Archives (document VI in this volume).

15. John Reid to Betsy Reid, April 1, 1814, John Reid Correspondence, LOC (document XIV in this volume).

16. John Donelson Jr. to Capt. John Donelson, April 1, 1814, Tennessee State Historical Society/Tennessee State Library and Archives, T-100, Misc. Collection (document IX in this volume).

17. Lt. Alexander McCulloch to Frances L. McCulloch, April 1, 1814, McCulloch Family Papers, University of Texas at Austin (document XII in this volume).

18. Andrew Jackson to Rachel Jackson, April 1, 1814, in Moser et al., *The Papers of Andrew Jackson*, 3:55 (document X in this volume).

19. Whether the remains of Daveiss were actually reinterred is a matter of dispute. See Otto A. Rothert, "The Grave of Joseph Hamilton Daveiss," *Filson Clue History Quarterly* 5 (October 1931): 191–96. For information on Daveiss, see John M. Trowbridge, "Kentuckians at the Battle of Tippecanoe," *Kentucky Ancestors* 41 (Spring 2006): 125–43. Montgomery's pistol now resides in the Smithsonian Institution's National Museum of American History.

20. For the memorialization of General Richard Montgomery, see Charles Royster, *A Revolutionary People at War: The Continental Army & American Character, 1775–1783* (Chapel Hill, N.C., 1996), 120–26.

21. A statue of Major Montgomery is located in front of the Montgomery County Courthouse. "Major Lemuel Purnell Montgomery—Montgomery, Alabama—Smithsonian Art Inventory Sculptures," Waymarking.com, April 12, 2012, http://www.waymarking.com/waymarks/WME73F_Major_Lemuel_Purnell_Montgomery_Montgomery_Alabama. Mitch Moulton and Robert Somerville also had Alabama cities named in their memory.

22. Albert J. Pickett, *History of Alabama, and Incidentally of Georgia and Mississippi*, 2 vols. (Charleston, S.C., 1851), 2:345 (second quotation) and 2:346 (first quotation). Pickett provided a complete physical description of the fallen major: "His eyes were keen and black; his hair was of a dark auburn color; his weight was one hundred and seventy-five pounds; his height was six feet and two inches, his form was admirably proportioned, and he was, altogether, the finest looking man in the army" (346).

23. Kanon, *Tennesseans at War*, 102.

24. Report of Andrew Jackson [to General Thomas Pinckney], April 5, 1814, *Nashville Whig*, May 25, 1814 (document XVII in this volume).

25. "Extract of a Letter from a Distinguished Officer, Dated 6 Miles from New Youchaw, March 29, 1814," *Clarion and Tennessee State Gazette*, April 12, 1814 (document II in this volume).

26. Initial reports indicated that Colonel Williams led the charge. The "first" man to make it to or over the barricade is a matter of some contention. In his report, Jackson singled out Colonel John Williams, as well as Montgomery. A secondhand report, collected by H. S. Halbert from an informant in 1885, asserted that James Love was the first to climb the breastwork and was severely wounded in the face by a tomahawk. There is no military record for a James Love in the extant muster rolls of the Thirty-Ninth Regiment, nor was he listed on the casualty report from the battle. Therefore, Halbert's information should be viewed with great skepticism. H. S Halbert, "Horse Shoe Incidents," Draper Manuscript Collection, Series YY, Tecumseh Papers, 101.

27. The quotation is from the cartouche of Isaac Stephens's "A Correct View of the Battle of the Horse Shoe," Gilder Lehrman Institute of American History, GLC06772.

28. Under the terms of the Treaty of Washington, 1832, all Creek land remaining in the borders of Alabama were allotted to individual heads of household after the land was surveyed. The battle site fell in T23N R23E, sections 15 and 22. The land was surveyed in January 1834. A Creek headman named Ken-no-ho-ce was allotted 156.5 acres in the southern half of section 15, which included Bean's Island. The remaining part of the bend, noted on the survey's mark as "Horse Shoe Bend and Battle Ground," was sold. The surveyor's field notes made no mention of the barricade or other signs of the battle. Original survey notes and survey plat, T23N R23E, Alabama Secretary of State, U.S. Land Office Field Notes, 1821–1845, Government Records Collection, Alabama Department of Archives and History, Montgomery, Ala. A version of the survey plat can also be found on the website maintained by the General Land Office Records, Bureau of Land Management, U.S. Department of the Interior: https://glorecords.blm.gov/details/survey/default.aspx?dm_id=66745&sid=bvnlkpox.bm5#surveyDetailsTabIndex=1.

29. *Wetumpka Argus*, June 26, 1839. The combat veteran was Samuel Barrett, likely the same Samuel S. Barrett who served as a corporal in Copeland's West Tennessee Militia. News reports did not identify the African American by name but related that he "stated he was in the battle and was owned by a gentleman in Tennessee at that time—that he came with the Tennessee troops, and saw major Montgomery buried." *Alabama Journal*, July 24, 1839. The African American was finally identified in 1901, when Dr. George W. Vines of Dadeville related that the militia party had been "guided by Americus Hammock, a negro who had been a musician (drummer or fifer) in Jackson's army at the battle of Horseshoe." *Montgomery Advertiser*, December 15, 1901. Vines knew the man's descendants. Albert J. Pickett procured written statements from two men who claimed to have been present: Private John Lovelady and Private Samuel Gearing. Lovelady has been identified as a member of the U.S. Thirty-Ninth. A John Lovelady appears in the compiled service files indexes as a private in Benton's Regiment of Tennessee volunteers (Second Regiment) and also Bunch's Regiment of East Tennessee Militia. Indexes to the Carded Records of Soldiers who served in Volunteer Organizations during the War of 1812, National Archives and Records Administration, Washington, D.C. No record has been located for Samuel Gearing. According to Pickett's records, the men asserted that the major had been buried about fifty yards from the barricade. Following the interment, brush was burned over the grave. See Peter Brannon, "Lemuel Purnell Montgomery," *Arrow Points* 8 (1924): 62–64. Neither were mentioned in contemporary news reports about the exhumation.

30. The Senate bill was amended to honor Montgomery "and others, officers and soldiers" who died during the battle. The bill apparently died in the House. *Journal of the Senate, at a Session of the General Assembly, of the State of Alabama Begun and Held in the City of Tuscaloosa, on the First Monday in December, 1839* (Tuscaloosa, Ala., 1840).

31. George L. Reaves, "Major Lemuel Purnell Montgomery His Death and Subsequent Removal from the Horseshoe Bend Battlefield," National Park Service, undated report; Historical Files, Folder 9F, Montgomery Commemorative Service.

32. *Columbus Ledger-Enquirer*, May 10–11, 1972 (quotations); *Dadeville Record*, April 27, 1972. By the time the NPS located the remains, they were merely large bone and skull fragments, along with teeth. Folder 9D, Montgomery Commemorative Service, Horseshoe Bend National Military Park files, Jackson's Gap, Ala.

33. *Montgomery Advertiser*, June 15, 2004.

34. John Frost, *Pictorial Life of Andrew Jackson, Embellished with Numerous Engravings* (Hartford, Conn., 1846).

35. The activities included participation by Horseshoe Bend National Military Park personnel, members of the Tennessee War of 1812 Bicentennial Commission, the Seventh U.S. Infantry Living History Association, the Tennessee Wars Commission, and the Tennessee Division, United States Daughters of the War of 1812.

36. Andrew Jackson to Rachel Jackson, April 1, 1814, in Moser et al., *The Papers of Andrew Jackson*, 4:55 (document X in this volume). Jackson was referring to Andrew Jackson Jr., one of Rachel's nephews whom Jackson and his wife adopted.

37. Americans were accused of mutilating the bodies of Shawnees, including that of Tecumseh, following the Battle of the Thames (1813) to make razor strops. If so, that would seem a more logical production than reins and may have been the inspiration for the bridle rein story, which comes from a questionable source from the late nineteenth century: the statement of an octogenarian who told Henry S. Halbert he had heard the story from veterans of the battle. "Incidents of the Battle of the Horse Shoe," by H. S. Halbert, Draper Manuscripts, YY: Tecumseh Papers #57. For "Tecumseh razor strops," see John Sugden, *Tecumseh: A Life* (New York, 1997), 379–80.

38. Horseshoe Bend National Military Park sought to obtain the item on loan for display at the park in 1972. Peter LaPaglia to Paul Ghioto, October 22, 1979, Folder 9F, Montgomery Commemorative Service, Horseshoe Bend National Military Park files, Jackson's Gap, Ala. The NPS made a concerted effort to locate a Creek war club (red stick) for display purposes. To date, no club definitively associated with the battle has been found. See Keith S. Hébert and Kathryn H. Braund, *Horseshoe Bend National Military Park Administrative History, a Report to the National Park Service, July 2019* (Daviston, Ala., 2019), 102–3.

39. "The Price of Freedom," National Museum of American History, Behring Center, http://amhistory.si.edu/militaryhistory/collection/object.asp?ID=524. Ironically, the text accompanying the pistol did not mention Horseshoe Bend but rather described the Battle of Talladega. This section of the exhibition has now been removed.

40. Judith Royster, "Indian Land Claims," in *Handbook of North American Indians*, vol. 2: *Indians in Contemporary Society*, ed. Garrick A. Bailey (Washington, D.C., 2008), 32.

41. For a discussion of the continuing commemoration and celebration of the victory at the Horseshoe during the Jacksonian era, see Justin Scott Weiss, "The Ghosts of Horseshoe Bend: Myth, Memory, and the Making of a National Battlefield" (MA thesis, Arizona State University, 2014), 26–46.

Chapter 5. Participant Accounts of the Battle of Horseshoe Bend

1. *Nashville Whig*, May 24, 1814.

2. Jackson followed with a fuller report on April 5, 1814, from Fort Williams. It was by that letter that Jackson sent Coffee's official report as well as a corrected map of the battlefield (document XVII in this volume).

3. Okfuskee was perhaps the largest town in the Upper Creek Nation aside from Tuckabatchee. The other towns listed, Okchai, Nuyaka, Hillabee, Thlathlagulgau (Fish Ponds), and Eufaula, were important Upper Creek towns located in the vicinity of Horseshoe Bend.

4. William McIntosh of Coweta was a leading war chief and supporter of the National Council faction against the Red Stick Creeks.

5. Ocheaupofau or Hickory Ground was located roughly two miles about the junction of the Coosa and Tallapoosa Rivers and was erroneously believed to be the site of another large contingent of Creek soldiers.

6. Carr is likely Captain Kerr, a contractor's agent in Captain Gordon's spies, who was killed. Captain Samuel Gaines, a member of Captain Parish's artillery company, died from wounds soon after the battle. Lewis, Dew, Laird, and Wilkinson were in Captain Parish's company of artillery.

7. Major John Reid was Jackson's aide-de-camp and wrote many of Jackson's letters.

8. The original sentence included a reference to Captain Benjamin Reynolds. The uncorrected original sentence read, "among the former were Maj Montgomery Lieut Somerville, & Lieut Moulton & Capt Reynolds, the three first who fell in the charge which was made on the works; & the last in attempting to oust a party of the enemy who had concealed themselves in the breast-work which terminated the lower extremity of the fortification." This correction occurred because Captain Benjamin Reynolds proved to be wounded but not mortally. He was discharged from the Thirty-Ninth in 1815.

9. Colonel Robert Hays served as the muster master for the Tennessee volunteers during the war. He was married to the sister of Rachel Jackson.

10. The letter was in care of "Capt. Smith."

11. Mary Caffery was the widowed sister-in-law of Andrew Jackson and lived at the Hermitage. Her son, John Caffery Jr., was known as Jack or Jacky.

12. Andrew Jackson Jr., one of the twins born to Rachel Jackson's brother and his wife, was adopted by the Jacksons.

13. Originally from Nashville, Perkins was the head of the Seventh Regiment of the Mississippi Territorial Militia, centered in Madison County. Frances C. Roberts, "The Public Square in Madison County History," *Huntsville Historical Review* 20 (Summer–Fall 1993): 8.

14. Tustanagee Thlucco, the Big Warrior, of Tuckabatchee was the leader of the Creek National Council.

15. John Walker Sr. was among four Cherokees appointed to the rank of major during the war.

16. Lewis was the quartermaster for the army.

17. A pole is 5.5 yards, therefore, 440 yards or roughly a quarter mile.

18. Webb was a private in Captain Moses Davis's Company of East Tennessee Militia, General Doherty's brigade. Davis offered the following testimony regarding Webb's experience: "I found the said Jessee Webb in a wounded situation trying to make his escape and as fast as he would get up he would fall headlong at his Length and I thought his falls would kill him I then took him by the arm to a place of safety and from the loss of blood and apparent wounds the said Webb then appeared to me could not survive." Statement by Captain Moses Davis, January 24, 1818, Jesse Webb Pension File. Jesse Webb, Veteran's Pension File, Invalid File 317, Records of the Veterans Administration, Record Group 15, National Archives and Records Administration, Washington, D.C.

19. General Anthony Wayne led an expedition into the Ohio Country in 1794, establishing Fort Defiance in the fall of 1794 at the confluence of the Auglaize and Maumee Rivers. His army defeated a coalition of northern tribes at the Battle of Fallen Timbers, August 20, 1794.

20. Mayfield had been captured by Creeks when he was ten years old and lived as a captive "nine or ten years." He then returned to his family in Nashville. When the war broke out, he joined the Americans and was invaluable to Jackson's forces as both a pilot and interpreter. House Report No. 147, 27th Congress, 2d Session (1842).

21. Cherokees who served became eligible to apply for pensions under terms of the treaty of 1835 (New Echota). Gideon Morgan provided evidence of Black Prince's service in the pension application noting "that Prince was proud of his service and made a fine soldier."

22. McKenney was superintendent of Indian Affairs from 1824 to 1830 and met several Creek survivors of the Creek War in 1825, when a Creek treaty delegation visited Washington, D.C., from whom he obtained much of his information. In his account, McKenney indicated that the Okfuskee prophet had predicted an attack from the rear and that when the Americans charged the breastwork, Menawa killed him for misleading them and harming the defensive effort. This part of McKenney's story makes no sense, for, indeed, the attack from the rear proved detrimental to the Red Stick defense and evacuation. Moreover, the Red Sticks and their prophets were clustered at the breastwork. This part of the narrative was either based on garbled accounts from the Creeks or perhaps meant by them in some way to discredit their prophets after the fact and explain their defeat at the barricade. Several accounts related that the Okfuskee prophet Monahee was killed by grapeshot at the barricade.

23. G. W. Grayson was among the most influential Muscogee Creek chiefs in the late nineteenth century. He was descended from Katy Grierson of Hillabee, whose family had opposed the Red Sticks. After the war, she married Johnie Benson.

Appendices

1. The editors of *The Papers of Andrew Jackson* incorrectly identified this "hasty sketch" mentioned by Jackson in his letter to Pinckney of March 28, 2814, as the map held by the Library of Congress. The Library of Congress map, designated as Cheatham Map #3 in appendix 1, is not a hasty sketch by an incomplete copy of Cheatham's map. The "hasty sketch" has not been located to date. See Harold D. Moser, David R. Hoth, Sharon Macpherson, and John H. Reinbold, eds., *The Papers of Andrew Jackson*, vol. 3: *1814–1815* (Knoxville, Tenn., 1991), 54n10.

Index